REVELATION

THE CLASSIC BIBLE BOOKS SERIES

The Song of Solomon: Love Poetry of the Spirit
Introduced and Edited by Lawrence Boadt; Foreword by John Updike

The Hebrew Prophets: Visionaries of the Ancient World
Introduced and Edited by Lawrence Boadt; Foreword by Desmond Tutu

The Great Sayings of Jesus: Proverbs, Parables and Prayers
Introduced and Edited by John Drane; Foreword by Richard Holloway

The Gospel of St John: The Story of the Son of God
Introduced and Edited by John Drane; Foreword by Piers Paul Read

The Book of Job: Why Do the Innocent Suffer?
Introduced and Edited by Lawrence Boadt; Foreword by Alice Thomas Ellis

Stories from the Old Testament: Volume I
Introduced and Edited by Lawrence Boadt; Foreword by Monica Furlong

Stories from the Old Testament: Volume II
Introduced and Edited by Lawrence Boadt; Foreword by Morris West

Revelation: The Apocalypse of St John
Introduced and Edited by John Drane; Foreword by Richard Harries

Forthcoming

Genesis: The Book of Beginnings
Introduced and Edited by Lawrence Boadt; Foreword by Sara Maitland

The Psalms: Ancient Poetry of the Spirit
Introduced and Edited by Lawrence Boadt and F. F. Bruce;
Foreword by R. S. Thomas

Sayings of the Wise: The Legacy of King Solomon
Introduced and Edited by Lawrence Boadt; Foreword by Libby Purves

The New Testament Epistles: Early Christian Wisdom
Introduced and Edited by John Drane; Foreword by Roger McGough

REVELATION
The Apocalypse of St John

INTRODUCED AND EDITED BY JOHN DRANE
FOREWORD BY RICHARD HARRIES

St. Martin's Griffin
New York

REVELATION: THE APOCALYPSE OF ST JOHN

ISBN 0-312-22513-X cloth
ISBN 0-312-22106-1 paperback

Library of Congress Cataloging-in-Publication Data

Revelation : the Apocalypse of St John / foreword by Richard Harries;
    introduction by John Drane.
        p. cm. -- (The Classic Bible series)
    Includes index.
    ISBN 0-312-22106-1
    1. Bible. N.T. Revelation--Criticism, interpretation, etc.
    I. Drane, John William. II. Series.
    BS2825.2.R39 1999
    228'.06--dc21
                                                            99-29991
                                                            CIP

First published in Great Britain by Lion Publishing plc, 1997.
First St. Martin's Griffin edition: September 1999
            10 9 8 7 6 5 4 3 2 1

Contents

ACKNOWLEDGMENTS

The text of 'Revelation in Literature' has been selected from *A Dictionary of Biblical Tradition in English Literature*, edited by David Lyle Jeffrey, copyright © 1992 by permission of Wm B. Eerdmans Publishing Co.

The unabridged text of Revelation has been taken from THE NEW JERUSALEM BIBLE. Copyright © 1985 by Doubleday, a division of Bantam Doubleday Dell Publishing Group, Inc. and Darton, Longman & Todd, Ltd. Used by permission of Doubleday, a division of Random House, Inc.

Three lines from 'An Ordinary Evening in New Haven' from COLLECTED POEMS by Wallace Stevens. Copyright 1950 by Wallace Stevens. Reprinted by permission of Alfred A Knopf Inc.

Foreword

For a modern reader the book of Revelation is strange, alien and often horrifying. Even the most talented producer of horror movies could hardly do justice to its bizarre, surreal imagery or the sheer terror of some of its themes.

Yet, at the same time, the book contains some of the most comforting pictures ever devised by the human imagination, many of which have entered deeply into our culture. For example, one passage that is often read at funerals comes from chapter 21:

> I saw a new heaven and a new earth: for the first heaven and the first earth were passed away... And God shall wipe away all tears from their eyes; and there shall be no more death, neither sorrow, nor crying, neither shall there be any more pain: for the former things are passed away. And he that sat upon the throne said, Behold, I make all things new. (Revelation 21:1, 4–5)

When a body is put into the grave the priest says:

> I heard a voice from heaven, saying unto me, write, from henceforth blessed are the dead which die in the Lord: even so saith the Spirit; for they rest from their labours.

This too comes from the book of Revelation (14:13).

For many, the heart of the book of Revelation is the worship of heaven. The imagery conveys a sense of sheer ecstasy, of people taken out of themselves in wonder, love and praise, with all the riches and art of the world coming to their appointed climax. People today find it difficult to understand worship. But the capacity to appreciate and admire, to wonder and praise, is fundamental to what it is to be a human being. Without this we become self-absorbed and cynical. Our capacity to be taken out of ourselves by that which is of real worth comes to its proper goal in the worship, the worth-ship, of God himself. This is a theme that runs through many chapters in the book.

For me, however, the starting point for entering into the book of Revelation is the fact that for so many the world is a cruel place.

Still there are people who are victimized and tortured for their beliefs. Still the poor, in their millions of millions, suffer. Still there is injustice and oppression on a massive scale. The innocent, not least the innocent children, cry out with those under the altar in the book of Revelation: 'How long, O Lord, how long?' Indeed it is not possible to begin to understand the book of Revelation without some sense of moral outrage against the world as it is at the moment.

With this starting point it is possible to see Revelation, for all the violence of its images, as offering something profoundly hopeful. For it is rooted in the conviction that in Jesus, all that is unjust, cruel or evil has in principle already been defeated and the final victory of God, including his victory over death, will be very soon. All that is contrary to the compassionate purpose of God will be smashed to smithereens. All who have remained true will be vindicated and will shine in an eternal light. The Hitlers, Stalins and Pol Pots of the world, together with the lesser bullies to be found in every street, do not have the last word. They will suffer what they have done to others.

The images of destruction in which this conviction is conveyed are shocking. But there is a, literally, redeeming feature. At the centre of divine power is the Lamb, the innocent one who voluntarily underwent death in order to redeem humanity. The gentle heart of God has borne in himself the consequences of creating a world such as ours and those who hold fast to him are saved for ever. From this faith rises the worship of God in heaven and on earth.

William Golding once defined himself as 'a universal pessimist but a cosmic optimist'. There is nothing so bad that it cannot get worse: and in some terrifying pictures the book of Revelation certainly bears that out. But in the end it offers a cosmic optimism.

Richard Harries

INTRODUCTION

Probably no book in the entire New Testament is less understood than the book of Revelation. All the great interpreters of the past had difficulty with it. Martin Luther found it an offensive piece of work, with very little to say about Christ – and John Calvin also had grave doubts about its value. Many modern readers feel the same way, and see its message as a return to superstitious mumbo-jumbo, and by implication a denial of the message of Jesus himself.

At the same time, there are others for whom the book of Revelation assumes far greater importance than many other books of the New Testament. They claim that it gives an insight into God's ultimate plans for humanity – even down to the details of how the present world will come to an end. So what can we make of it? Does it have any lasting significance, or is it to be dismissed as an unfortunate mistake by the early church, which should never have been included among the books of the New Testament?

A Christian Book?

When we look at the book of Revelation in detail, it is clear that its author shares with the rest of the New Testament a positive emphasis on God's involvement in human affairs. Though the language and imagery in which he writes is apocalyptic in form, his message has a distinctive Christian emphasis.

Unlike every other apocalyptic book, Revelation names both its author and its first readers. It was written by a person called John, and was sent 'From John to the seven churches in the province of Asia' (Revelation 1:4), in the towns of Ephesus, Smyrna, Pergamum, Thyatira, Sardis, Philadelphia and Laodicea. These churches are addressed in quite specific terms, and incidents and individuals are mentioned by name. This kind of self-confidence was never shared by Jewish apocalyptic writers, who were generally so afraid of their persecutors that to have identified themselves in this way would have led to certain death. Of course, some members of these churches were also being persecuted, but that was no reason for disguising the true nature of their Christian faith.

Even in those parts of the book that are most similar to earlier Jewish writings, John's visions are always closely linked to his experience of life in the church. His visions come to him 'on the Lord's day', and contain many references to the worship of the church: its confessions of faith, prayers and hymns.

Revelation looks forward to a future intervention of God in the affairs of this world. But its understanding of this is different from that of earlier Jewish apocalyptists. Without exception, they regarded this world and all its affairs as irretrievably evil. History was a meaningless enigma, and the sooner its course was stopped, the better. In this respect, apocalyptic writing was a departure from the mainstream faith of the Old Testament. There, the prophets had looked forward to the coming of a 'Day of the Lord', when God would intervene in a final and decisive way in the affairs of the world. But they always regarded this as the continuation of what God was already doing in the present order of things. The God who would inaugurate a new world order in the future could also be known here and now in the events of human life.

Apocalyptic writers rejected this view, because they could make no sense of their own present experience. But the book of Revelation follows the Old Testament in making a clear link between what God is doing in history now, and what will come in the future. Indeed, the entire meaning of God's plan for the future of humanity is to be found in a historical event – the life, death and resurrection of Jesus, 'the Lamb of God'. And far from the suffering of Christians being a meaningless interlude, John declares that it is one of the most powerful responses against all forms of evil.

Revelation therefore does not follow slavishly the pattern of its Jewish apocalyptic predecessors. It presents a distinctively Christian explanation of the presence of evil in the affairs of human life. Its message might be expressed through conventional Jewish language and imagery, but its content goes beyond the literary form of apocalyptic writing.

The Book and its Message

The first chapters of Revelation are similar to many other New Testament writings: they contain seven letters to seven churches in the Roman province of Asia. They are not real letters like those written by Paul, for they purport to come from the risen Jesus himself. John says their content was given to him in a vision, just like the rest of the book. But they deal with very down-to-earth matters, and show a detailed knowledge of these communities and their environment. The churches were involved in disputes over Christian belief. Their commitment to Christ was wavering, and as a result they were in no position to face up to the challenge of state persecution. To do that, they needed to be wholeheartedly committed. This message is found many times in the New Testament (e.g. in letters such as 1 Peter).

But the second part of the book is quite different. Here we come face to face with the language and imagery of apocalyptic writings. The visions no longer relate to real events and people. Instead, they introduce monsters and dragons in a quick succession of terrifying events. The whole section is introduced in chapters four and five by a vision of heaven which sets the scene for what follows. Here the author explains the basic way in which he understands God's workings in history. God is 'high and exalted' in absolute majesty and holiness, and men and women (represented by the twenty-four elders in the divine court) find their true significance as they worship and serve God. Even then, they are quite incapable of reflecting every aspect of God's personality, and when a sealed scroll is produced, containing God's revelation to the world, the elders are unable to open it to reveal its contents. After an angel has searched unsuccessfully in heaven, on earth and in the underworld, God's own heavenly deliverer appears on the scene – the Lamb of God, Jesus Christ.

This is a powerful and impressive presentation of the central importance of the life, death and resurrection of Jesus in the Christian understanding of the cosmos and its meaning, and at the very beginning of his visions, John links the future destiny of the world and its inhabitants with the revelation of God through the historical events of the life of Jesus.

The chapters that follow then present a series of visions describing how God's opponents will all be judged. Many of the descriptions here are quite horrific, and much of the language in which God's judgment is described comes from the story of the plagues in Egypt in the Old Testament book of Exodus. This gives us a clue to the point that John is making. For in the exodus story, God's main purpose had not been the plagues. They were merely a prelude to the salvation that God had planned for the people of Israel – and through them, for the whole world. So too in Revelation, the main point of the book is not to be found in God's judgment upon evil, but in the conviction that God is now in the process of making a new world from which evil will be completely banished. In this new world, men and women will enjoy a new and unfettered freedom to know God in a direct way: 'God will make his home among them... he will wipe away all tears from their eyes; there will be no more death, and no more mourning or sadness or pain. The world of the past has gone.' (Revelation 21:3-4).

There have been many attempts to arrange the visions of Revelation according to some sort of outline. One of the most attractive suggestions was first put forward by the German scholar Ernst Lohmeyer. He suggested that, with the exception of chapters four and five, and the description of the new heavens and earth, the whole book is arranged in a pattern of seven sections of sevens:

Seven seals (6:1 – 8:1)
Seven trumpets (8:2 – 11:19)
Seven visions of the dragon and his kingdom (12:1 – 13:18)
Seven visions of the Lamb of God and his coming
   (14:1–20)
Seven bowls of God's anger against evil (15:1 – 16:21)
Seven visions of the fall of 'Babylon' (17:1 – 19:10)
Seven visions of the end (19:11 – 21:4)

What we have in these visions is a kaleidoscopic picture of how God will finally overcome the powers of evil. It is the work not of a self-conscious theologian but of a great artist, and like a good artist John depicts the same subject from a number of different perspectives, in order to reinforce the overall impression that he wants to create.

Making Sense of the Message

It is difficult today to understand fully every detail of these visions. But their impact on the original readers of the book of Revelation can readily be appreciated. John assured his Christian readers that their present suffering was only temporary. Their great enemy 'Babylon' – a term which John, like Peter, used to refer cryptically to Rome – would ultimately come under the judgment of God. Injustice and evil would not be allowed to win out, for God alone is the Lord of history. The destiny of nations, as well as of individuals, is in God's personal control.

This view of Revelation is sometimes called the 'Preterist' view of Revelation (from the Latin word praeteritum, 'referring to the past'), and it is a widely held view. But over the centuries, other readers of the New Testament, fascinated by the intriguingly mysterious character of Revelation's message, have refused to accept that its significance can be exhausted just by seeing what it meant for those Christians to whom it was first addressed. Some of the Church Fathers regarded it as a symbol of the great truths of the Christian faith. Origen and Augustine thought of its imagery as a symbolic account of the principles of God's working throughout history. They saw its weird descriptions of persons and battles and beasts not as real events, but as a dramatic presentation of the age-long opposition between God and the forces of evil. This way of understanding Revelation undoubtedly helps to make sense of many of the most difficult passages in the book, and it also succeeds in relating it to the needs of its first readers – for they needed to be assured of the successful outcome of the struggle in which they were engaged.

But in the last 100 years or more, a large body of popular opinion has come to look at Revelation in a different way. 'Futurist' interpreters argue that its real meaning is connected with events that are still in the future even now, and its full significance will become plain only to that generation which finds itself living in 'the last days'. Some have even suggested that the seven letters with which the book opens are not real letters at all, but part of a detailed clairvoyant insight given to John, describing seven successive ages of church history, reaching from the 1st century up to the end of time. Many of these are also 'Dispensationalists', believing that we today have reached the stage of the seventh and final letter (to Laodicea); so, they claim, our own generation is living at the very end of world history. There are many difficulties with views like this.

There is the plain fact that several generations have believed themselves to be living in the last days – some even putting a date on the end of the world. But they have all been wrong.

More serious is the fact that Jesus himself explicitly warned his disciples not to indulge in this kind of speculation: 'No one knows ... when that day and hour will come – neither the angels in heaven, nor the Son; the Father alone knows.' In light of that, it is hardly likely that God would have given the information only to a select band of modern readers of the book of Revelation!

Another serious objection is that according to this view, the book of Revelation must have been totally meaningless and irrelevant to the people for whom it was ostensibly written. If the letters to the churches of Asia were not real letters, related to the concerns of real people, that would make Revelation quite different from every other book in the whole of the Bible. It also shares the general pessimism about existence in this world that was a hallmark of Jewish apocalyptic literature – but which was quite foreign to New Testament thinking. The early church was not offering 'pie in the sky', but claimed to enjoy a living, personal relationship with God through Jesus Christ here and now in this present life.

The whole New Testament presents the clear conviction that there will be a point at which God must deal decisively with the forces of evil – and then the new society of peace and justice announced by Jesus will become a lasting and tangible reality. But there is no justification for regarding either Revelation or any other book of the Bible as a kind of blueprint for the future course of world events.

The Author and Date of Revelation

Revelation is the only New Testament book that was dated by the Church Fathers. According to Irenaeus, John saw his vision 'not long ago, but almost in our own generation, towards the end of Domitian's reign' (Against Heresies 5.30.3).

This corresponds quite closely with what can be discerned from the concerns of the book. Domitian (AD81–96) required all citizens to worship him as a test of their political allegiance. Naturally, Christians did not want to be disloyal citizens – but neither were they prepared to offer worship to the emperor. As a result, many of them were persecuted and hounded to death as enemies of the state.

Some argue that Revelation is to be set earlier, in the days just after the persecution of Christians by Nero. But Nero's persecution did not, so far as we know, involve the demand for emperor-worship. This objection can be avoided by suggesting that the author of Revelation had been in Rome during Nero's time, and saw worse to come, so he wrote his book to the Christians of Asia Minor not so much as an encouragement in the face of actual persecution, but as a warning of what they could expect soon. It has also been claimed that careful analysis of the possible identities of the seven emperors listed in 17:9–11 leads to the time of Nero or his successor Galba (AD68–69). But this assumes that John had actual historical figures in mind at this point, whereas it is just as likely that the seven emperors were not meant to be real people, but just the sum total of all the evil that is opposed to God.

On balance, there is no compelling reason to reject the traditional date for Revelation of about AD95.

The author of Revelation was a person called John. St Justin Martyr describes him as 'one of the apostles of Christ' (Dialogue with Trypho the Jew, 91). But many students of the New Testament find that hard to accept. The writer of Revelation seems to mention 'the twelve apostles of the Lamb' as a group that was quite separate from his own experience (21:14), and the way he writes of himself as 'your brother... a follower of Jesus... your partner' (1:9) hardly suggests he was a person of great authority in the church. He was however clearly steeped in the imagery of Jewish apocalyptic writings, and we may therefore suppose he was a Jew.

At the same time, there are a number of unusual connections between Revelation and the Gospel of John. Both John and Revelation refer to Jesus as 'the word [logos] of God' (John 1:1–14; 1 John 1:1–4; Revelation 19:11–16). Both of them also call Jesus 'the Lamb of God', though they use different Greek words to do so (John 1:29;

Revelation 5:6–14). In addition, both the Gospel and the letters of John seem to have had some connection with the city of Ephesus – and that was one of the churches addressed in Revelation.

In view of all this, some have suggested that there was at Ephesus a 'school' of Christian thinkers established and inspired by John the apostle – and perhaps different members of this group, including John himself, were responsible for the final form of the various books which now go under his name.

John Drane

REVELATION IN
<u>LITERATURE</u>

Themes and Images

Themes and Images

Alpha and Omega

Scriptural reference to *alpha* and *omega*, the first and last letters of the Greek alphabet, is confined to Revelation, in which God twice asserts, 'I am the Alpha and the Omega, the beginning and the end' (1:8; 21:6), and Christ once declares, 'I am the Alpha and the Omega, the beginning and the end, the first and the last' (22:13). (The King James Version's use of the phrase again in Revelation 1:11 is not warranted by the manuscripts.) The use of alpha and omega to denote God's eternity and infinitude is rooted in such Old Testament texts as Isaiah 44:6 (cf. 41:4; 48:12), 'I am the first, and I am the last; and beside me there is no God'; but it is probable that the Johannine locution itself is derived, by analogy, from rabbinic tradition, where aleph and tau, the first and last letters of the Hebrew alphabet, express a parallel symbolic sense: for example, 'My Saints... are the sons of men who have kept the whole Law from Aleph to Taw' (Shabbethai 55a on Ezekiel 9:6). Most authorities also point out that the Hebrew word for 'truth' is composed of the first, middle, and last letters of the alphabet.

There is, it seems, no precedent for the application of alpha and omega to Christ in Revelation 22:13, although it is this text which becomes the mainstay of subsequent tradition. Both Greek and Latin Fathers draw attention to it as affirming the divinity of Christ.

In antiquity and the Middle Ages, alpha and omega occur more frequently in Christian art and inscriptions than in literature. With few exceptions, Christian iconography employs the letters on coins, vases, and monuments in connection with figures symbolic of Christ (rather than God the Father), the usual form being a monogram of *Christos* flanked by alpha and omega.

In English literature, from the Middle Ages to the end of the 18th century, there are oblique allusions, as in Milton's *Paradise Lost* (5.165) but no explicit references in any of the major poets. In the 19th century, by contrast, allusions abound, although often cut adrift from traditional christological moorings. The sacred river Alph (=

Alpha or Aleph) meanders though Coleridge's *Kubla Khan*, and Wordsworth in a pantheistic effusion in *The Prelude* (1805) construes alpine scenery in imagery invoking Revelation, as

> Characters of the great Apocalypse,
> The types and symbols of Eternity,
> Of first, and last, and midst, and without end. (6.638–40)

In Charlotte Brontë's *Jane Eyre*, thorough secularization is evident in Rochester's confession that 'the Alpha and Omega of my heart's wishes broke involuntarily from my lips in the words – "Jane! Jane! Jane!"' (chapter 37).

In 20th-century literature, alpha and omega symbolize a variety of beginnings and endings, religious and secular, apocalyptic and mundane, serious and comic. In the 'Proteus' episode of Joyce's *Ulysses*, Stephen Dedalus, cynical and dépaysé, imagines finding his roots by placing a call on the umbilical telephone network that connects him back to Mother Eve: 'Hello. Kinch here. Put me on to Edenville. Aleph, alpha: nought, nought, one.' In Wallace Stevens' private mythology in *An Ordinary Evening in New Haven* (canto 6, long version), 'Naked Alpha' balances 'the hierophant Omega' as antagonistic 'interpreters of life' in the poet's exploration of 'plain reality':

> But that's the difference: in the end and the way
> To the end. Alpha continues to begin.
> Omega is refreshed at every end.

In the Neoplatonic anthropology of Teilhard de Chardin, the Omega Point is the imagined moment in human evolution where biogenesis yields to nougenesis, where body yields to mind: 'We reach the Omega Point when we attain to the Hyper-Personal' (*Phenomenon of Man*, 4.2). More pessimistically, the mutant human remnant of a nuclear holocaust in *Beneath the Planet of the Apes* (1970), first sequel to Pierre Boulle's *Planet of the Apes* (1967), worships an ICBM carrying a cobalt bomb, with A and Ω depicted on the rocket's fins.

John Spencer Hill
University of Ottawa

Book of Life

In the Revelation to St John on Patmos are found three references to the book of life, where it refers to a great ledger read out on the Day of Judgment from the throne of God (Revelation 20:12–15).

The only Old Testament use of the complete expression is found in Psalm 69:28, but God's book in Exodus 32:32 is clearly antecedent, as are similar 'books' referred to in Psalm 139:16, Isaiah 4:3, and Malachi 3:16. It is in Daniel that the idea of a book (or books) as the basis upon which final judgment is to be made is most thoroughly developed (Daniel 7:10, 12); the same notion recurs in other apocalyptic writing (e.g., Ethiopic Enoch 47:3; 108:3; Jubilees 30:20–22; 36:10; 39:6). Midrash Tannaim regards the book of God referred to by Moses in Exodus 32 as the book of eternal life in which are enrolled all the faithful.

Perhaps the most remarkable English poem on this subject, *The Last Judgment (Christ III)*, creates a powerful scene (drawn on Matthew 24, Isaiah 13, and Mark 13) in which each sinner is revealed to himself by the light of the Cross: Christ crucified for the sins of the world is raised up to tower over the whole of the universe and the implicit call to remembrance in each life is by way of a question about one's response to Calvary. But the trace of the 'book of life' is then introduced in phrases which speak of how the damned 'shall find reward / Befitting their record of words and works' (1363–64), and Augustine's notion that the 'books' of Revelation 20:12 are the Old Testament and New Testament construed as Divine Word is echoed in the summary reflection of the poet on the damned: 'They broke God's word, / The Books' bright bidding' (1628–29).

In Aelfric's Sermon for Ascension Eve he quotes Revelation 3:5, observing that the names of 'all those persons who are to come into the kingdom of God are written in the book of life *(liflican bec)* and we shall with zeal *(geornfulness)* and with good works find that our names too are written there' (ed. Pope, *Homilies of Aelfric*, 25.757.15–19). In the Towneley 'Judgment' pageant (no. 30) it is the devils who, on hearing the last 'trumpet' sound, hasten to gather books of reckoning, 'rentals' (134) which record the sins of all mankind.

The Book of Margery Kempe records her vision of an angel who, despite the traditional reservation expressed in Revelation 5:9, shows her the 'Book of Life,' in which she discovers her own name written. There follows the record of a revelation in which Jesus speaks to her, confirming that her name is 'written at the Trinity's foot' in the Book, for which reason she is entitled to be 'right merry' (chapter 85). Dante, in his final apocalyptic vision in the *Paradiso*, speaks of an 'Eternal Light' in whose depth he sees ingathered 'bound by love in a single volume, that which is dispersed in leaves throughout the universe' *(legato con amore in un volume, / ciò che per l'universo si squaderna)* – clearly related to the book of life (33.85–87).

Exodus 32:32 evidently lies behind the reference in *Richard 2*, where Shakespeare has Mowbray say to his colleague in exile, Bolingbroke, 'If ever I were traitor, / My name be blotted from the book of life, / And I from Heaven banished as from hence!' (1.3.201–03). The books and book, singular and plural, are set in relation to one another by John Donne in his *Meditation 17*, in a passage reminiscent of Dante:

> All mankind is of one author and is one volume; when one man dies, one chapter is not torn out of the book, but translated into a better language; and every chapter must be so translated. God employs several translators; some pieces are translated by age, some by sickness, some by war, some by justice; but God's hand is in every translation, and his hand shall bind up all our scattered leaves again for that library where every book shall lie open to one another.

Byron's Manfred, weighed down with his sense of responsibility to a final reckoning, exclaims, 'My days are numbered, and my deeds recorded' *(Manfred*, 3.4.314). But the weighty force of the biblical image in medieval and Renaissance literature is unmatched in usage after the Enlightenment generally speaking. Typically the book of life is invoked in analogy with something of less moment, or psychologized. In Thomas de Quincey's *Suspina de Profundis* those like the Pariah, the Jew, and the English criminal are 'blotted out from the books of remembrance in sweet far-off England', and in the same writer's *Confessions of an Opium Eater*, the drug prompts *la recherche du temps perdus*, suggesting to de Quincey that 'the dread book of account which the Scriptures speak of is, in fact, the mind of each individual'. A similar allusion may be found in Dickens' *David Copperfield* (chapter 38); in Conrad's *Outcast of the Islands* drowned sailors go to their watery grave 'without needing to open the book of life, because they could look at eternity reflected on the element that gave the life and dealt the death' (1.2). In Tennyson's 'Sea Dreams' books of financial accounting are connected to ultimate accountability. A young man who has been defrauded asks to see the records of his oppressor and, when unsuccessful, reflects wistfully that 'When the great Books – see Daniel seven and ten – / Were opened, I should find he meant me well'. In *Sesame and the Lilies* Ruskin observes that while some in his generation no longer believe in immortality, others anticipate that 'within these five, or ten, or twenty years, for every one of us the judgment will be set, and the books opened' ('The Mystery of Life and its Arts').

David L. Jeffrey
University of Ottawa

Celestial City

The book of Revelation concludes with St John's vision of the 'holy city, new Jerusalem, coming down from God out of heaven, prepared as a bride adorned for her husband'. A 'great voice out of heaven' addressed John regarding the celestial city (Revelation 21:2–5):

> Behold, the tabernacle of God is with men, and he will dwell with them, and they shall be his people, and God himself shall be with them, and be their God. And God shall wipe away all tears from their eyes; and there shall be no more death, neither sorrow, nor crying, neither shall there be any more pain: for the former things are passed away. And he that sat upon the throne said, 'Behold, I make all things new'.

This passage, reminiscent of the vision of Ezekiel (Ezekiel 40:1–4; 48:35) looks forward to a time when the fallen creation will be completely renewed. The holy city, descending from heaven, will be suspended over the earth and filled with such divine radiance that it has 'no need of the sun, neither of the moon to shine in it'

(Revelation 21:23). In the New Jerusalem the people of God are in unity at last (21:22, 24), having no need for a Temple because the 'temple is the Lord God the Almighty and the Lamb' (21:22). Familiar and even hallowed symbols have passed away as shadows, pale simulacra beside the glory of God's actual presence.

St Augustine's famous commentary on this passage in *De civitate Dei* declares the basic understanding of the Church that this vision concerns not the historical 'city set on a hill,' but the future dwelling of the 'immortality and eternity of the saints' following the Last Judgment. The celestial Jerusalem he calls the *visio pacis* of the Christian pilgrim, glimpsed only from afar in this life, but at last 'to come down out of heaven, because the grace with which God formed it is of heaven' (*De civitate Dei*, 20.19.17).

Chaucer's Parson provides for pilgrims and readers of *The Canterbury Tales* an Augustinian analogy between the pilgrimage from Southwark to Canterbury and the spiritual journey from Babylon to 'Jerusalem celestial,' a 'viage' through history and out of time to eternal felicity, 'the endelees blisse of hevene':

> there joye hath no contrarioustee of wo ne grevaunce; ther alle harmes been passed of this present lyf, ther as is the sikernesse fro the peyne of helle, ther as is the blisful compaignye that rejoysen hem everemo everich of otheres joye, / ther as the body of man that whilom was foul and derk is moore cleer than the sonne, ther as the body that whilom was syk, freele, and fieble, and mortal, is inmortal, and so strong and so hool that there may nothing apeyren it, / there as ne is neither hunger, thurst, ne coold, but every soule replenyssed with the sighte of the parfit knowynge of God. (*Canterbury Tales*, 10.1076–79)

The vision of the celestial city set on a 'cliff' afforded by the *Pearl* Poet begins with its physical characteristics – walls and gates of jewels and pearls (2.60ff.). Interpretation of these features from St John's vision develops through the Pearl Maiden's Beatrice-like instruction concerning the state of the blessed, in which all the conditions described in Revelation 21 are detailed in turn (cf. Dante, *Paradiso*, 30.59–122). Such conventional descriptions, owing directly to the passage in Revelation, are frequently adumbrated by phrases from medieval Latin hymns on the celestial Jerusalem, including the anonymous *'Jerusalem Luminosa'* and *'Urbs Beata Jerusalem'* as well as the *'Ad Perennis Vitae Fontem'* of St Peter Damian and *'De Contemptu Mundi'* of St Bernard of Cluny, which concludes with a glorious vision of 'Jerusalem the Golden'. (The hymn of this title by the Scots writer David Dickson, 1583–1663, is a kind of loose cento of these Latin hymns.)

The goal of 'liberating' the literal Jerusalem (and establishing, perhaps, its celestial counterpart) was a preoccupation of some of the crusades. The idealistic and millennialist aspect of medieval military expeditions still hovers in the background of Tasso's enormously influential 16th-century epic, *Gerusalemme Liberata* (1580; English translation by R. Carew, 1594, and by E. Fairfax, 1600). In Spenser's contemporary English epic, *The Faerie Queene*, Redcrosse Knight is led to 'the highest Mount' and 'a goodly City... whose wals and towres were builded high and strong / Of perle and precious stone' – a synthesis of Sinai, the Mount of Olives, and Parnassus which is nonetheless finally identified by the 'godly aged Sire' as

> The New Hierusalem, that God has built
> For those to dwell in, that are chosen his,
> His chosen people purg'd from sinful guilt
> With pretious blood. (1.10.57–61)

In the Reformation period John's vision of the New Jerusalem is given extensive literal and spiritual interpretation. Various features of the historical Jerusalem – for example, its being set on a hill (cliff, or tableland) – are blended with the details in Revelation in describing heaven or the millennial reign of Christ and his saints. John Bale's *A comedy concernynge thre lawes* projects that after the exhaustion of human moral suffering will come the new heaven of renewed faith and the new earth of mankind's understanding of that faith. Sir David Lindsay's poem *The Monarchie* (1553), possibly inspired by a sermon of John Knox, presents a 'history' of the world from Creation to Last Judgment and imagines how 'Heven renewit salbe, than / Rychtso, the erth, with devyse / Compair tyll hevinlye Paradyse' (6055–57), with the millennial kingdom passing in an hour, because in effect all those present for the second coming will be immortal and eternally

24

preserved at the age of thirty-three. Sir Walter Raleigh's *History of the World* (1614) similarly speaks of the descent of the New Jerusalem as the culmination of history.

The tracts and texts of political utopianism in the 17th century often envisioned temporally realized versions of the New Jerusalem – both in England and abroad. The dissenters who fled their homeland and settled the (apocalyptically named) New World also saw in John's Apocalypse a pertinent revelation of their own destiny, imagining, in the words of Johnson's *Wonder-Working Providence*, that 'this is the place where the Lord will create a new Heaven and a new Earth in, new Churches, and a new Commonwealth together'. John Cotton called his brethren to 'Awake, awake, put on thy strength, O New English Zion and put on thy Beautiful Garments, O American Jerusalem'. For Cotton Mather, 'AMERICA is legible' in biblical promises of the New Jerusalem.

In devotional literature of the period, the New Jerusalem bespeaks a spiritual rather than a political realm. Jeremy Taylor's 'A Meditation of Heaven' contemplates that city

> Where the great King's transparent throne
> Is of an entire jasper stone;
> There the eye
> O' the chrysolite,
> And a sky
> Of diamonds, rubies, chrysoprase,
> And above all thy holy face
> Makes an eternal clarity.

Among the best known of such meditations on the hereafter is Richard Baxter's *Saints' Everlasting Rest*, in the 16th and final chapter of which Revelation 21 provides the basis of a striking contrast between the 'way of the wilderness... that howling desert' and

> thy Father's glory... the glorious new Jerusalem, the gates of pearl, the foundation of pearl, the streets and pavement of transparent gold. That sun which lighteth all the world will be useless there; even thyself shall be as bright as yonder shining sun. God will be the sun, and Christ the light, and in his light thou shalt have light.

Baxter's vision is essentially that of Bunyan, whose *Pilgrim's Progress* has as its goal, at the culmination of a journey prompted by grace and carried out in perseverance, 'the City [which] stood upon a mighty hill, Mount Sion, the heavenly Jerusalem'. Bunyan's pilgrim will there join 'the innumerable company of Angels, and the Spirits of Just Men made perfect in the Paradise of God,' his angel hosts tell him, where he shall 'see the Tree of Life, and eat of the never-fading fruits thereof'.

One of the best-known English hymns on the subject of the New Jerusalem is John Newton's 'Glorious things of thee are spoken, / Zion, city of our God,' based principally on Isaiah 33:20–21. Blake's *Jerusalem: the Emanation of the Giant Albion* mixes biblical prophecy with social criticism, looking to the historical realization of the heavenly kingdom, in which the giant England will awake from its vegetable slumber to eternal life when at last 'Jerusalem is called Liberty among the Children of Albion' (3.54.5). Similar sentiments are expressed in Blake's well-known prefatory poem to *Milton*, beginning, 'And did those feet in ancient time / Walk upon England's mountains green?' and ending,

> I will not cease from Mental Fight
> Nor shall my Sword sleep in my hand
> Till we have built Jerusalem
> In England's green & pleasant Land.

It is not a utopian social vision but rather a yearning to be free of the world which prompts Anne Bradstreet's extensive quotation of Revelation 21 in 'The Flesh and the Spirit,' which begins, 'The City which I hope to dwell / There's none on earth can parallel'. Similarly, in Hawthorne's *The Scarlet Letter,* Dimmesdale discourses of 'saintly men, who walk with God on earth' and 'would fain be away! To walk with him on the golden pavements of the New Jerusalem' (chapter 9; cf. Genesis 5:22). This passage is reminiscent of another homiletical invocation (here of Revelation 21:27) in Sir Walter Scott's *Kenilworth*, in which Foster discusses the exposition of Master Holdforth with Doctor Alasco, observing that 'the Holy Writ says that the gold and precious stones are in no sort for those who work abominations, or who frame lies' (chapter 22). In Whittier's 'The Pageant,' winter's 'wild work of frost and light' becomes a 'foregleam of the Holy City / Like that to him on Patmos given, / The white bride coming down from heaven!'

Nineteenth-century references in English literature range from sentimentality to cynical debunking. Exemplary of the former is Sabine Baring-Gould's 'The City God hath Made,' which has its 'foundation-stones' in 'the beauteous fields of Eden' and in which the standard species of an English country garden somewhat overgrow the crystal river and golden pavements. Christina Rossetti wonders, 'What will it be at last to see a 'holy' city! For Londoners, for Parisians, for citizens of all cities upon earth, to see a holy city!' In Wilde's *De Profundis*, 'Far off, like a perfect pearl, one can see the city of God. It is so wonderful that it seems as if a child could reach it in a summer's day.' Tennyson's 'Ode on the Death of... Wellington' talks about the warrior as a spiritual pilgrim who

> ... with toil of heart and knees and hands
> Thro' the long gorge to the far light has won
> His path upward, and prevail'd
> Shall find the toppling crags of Duty scaled
> Are close upon the shining table lands
> To which our God himself is moon and sun.

Hardy's narrator in *Jude the Obscure* recasts the vision somewhat:

> Through the solid barrier of cold cretaceous upland to the northward he was always beholding a gorgeous city – the fancied place he had likened to the New Jerusalem, though there was perhaps more of the painter's imagination and less of the diamond merchant's in his dreams thereof than in those of the Apocalyptic writer. (1.3)

David L. Jeffrey
University of Ottawa

Dragon

In Revelation 12:3 there appears in the heavens 'a great red dragon, having seven heads and ten horns and seven crowns upon his heads'.

All the ancient mythologies (e.g., that of BelMarduk) contain such a dragon creature – usually serpentine in body, hydra-headed, and winged – which embodies the wild forces of chaos and destruction against which a cosmic conflict must be fought. The slaying of the dragon restores order and brings blessedness.

In the prophetic literature of the Old Testament the 'dragon' (King James Version, from *tannin*, 'sea monster') represents all hostile and arrogant powers which rise up against the Lord and are subdued by him (Isaiah 27:1; 51:9–10; Jeremiah 51:34; Ezekiel 29:3; 32:2). In Bel and the Dragon, an apocryphal addition to the book of Daniel which appears in the Septuagint text (chapter 14), the dragon worshipped by the Babylonians is fed balls of hair mixed with tar and fat, a concoction which demonstrates the dragon's mere mortality.

Later rabbinical commentators incorporated the supernatural monsters Behemoth and Leviathan of Job 40–41 into this tradition (Baba Batra 75a; Alphabetot 98; Pirqe Mashiah 76). In the Jewish messianic programme these monsters are to be released to wreak havoc on the human race until finally slain by the will of God (Apocalypse of Baruch 29.4); thereafter they are to be consumed in the messianic banquet (Tehillim 18.153; 23.202).

Revelation is the only New Testament book which takes up the dragon motif. In two passages (Revelation 12:9; 20:2) the dragon is explicitly identified with 'the ancient serpent, he who is called the devil and Satan,' and so takes its place in the gallery of Christian images as the source and personification of all evil as well as the monster of darkness and chaos. In chapter 12 the author of Revelation describes a vision which incorporates the ancient tale of enmity between the serpent/dragon and the woman (see Genesis 3:15) in new terms. It may also reflect an ancient astronomical pattern of the conflict between Scorpio and Virgo (cf. Virgil, *Georgics*, 1.32) and the myth of a prince whom the usurper tries to kill at birth but who is providentially snatched away and hidden until in maturity he kills the usurper and takes the throne. In biblical terms the sun-clothed woman gives birth to the Messiah, who is exposed to Satanic dangers until he is taken up into heaven, whence he will return in triumph.

Immediately after this cosmic battle with the dragon, two beasts appear, one from the sea and one from the land; both exercise the power of the dragon (Revelation 13:1–18). They have affinities with the four beasts of Daniel 7, the first beast combining characteristics of all four. A generally accepted interpretation is that these two beasts represent Roman imperial power, which – for the province of Asia – came up annually 'out of the sea' with the arrival of the proconsul at Ephesus and the local *Commune Asiae*, which managed the imperial cult and exercised the delegated power of Rome in local government (see Revelation 13:12–16). In chapter 17 the first monster returns in the form of the scarlet beast, once more with seven heads and ten horns, being ridden by the Whore of Babylon. Here its identification with imperial power is made clear by the reference to the seven hills of Rome (17:9).

While many commentators, for example, Tyconius in the 4th century, have seen the dragon image as embodying the cosmic force of evil to be fought in all ages, others have identified the dragon and the two beasts with historical forces or persons. Many examples of the first interpretation are to be found in medieval art, where either Christ or St Michael is represented trampling the dragon. Psalm 91:13 – 'the dragon shalt thou trample under feet' – gave rise to numerous allied legends of the slaying of dragons by saints (cf. *Glossa Ordinaria*, *Patrologia Latina*, 113.1000). The most widely known version of this conflict is enacted in the legend of St George of Cappadocia (named patron saint of England after 1222) and his victory over the dragon, echoes of which are found both in the 14th-century alliterative *Morte d'Arthur* and Malory's version of the following century.

From the beginning, however, interpretive imagination has been focused on the identification of the dragon's seven heads and, most famous of all biblical puzzles, the solution to 'the number of the beast,' as propounded in Revelation 13:18: 'Here is wisdom. Let him that hath understanding count the number of the beast: for it is the number of a man; and his number is Six hundred threescore and six.' The seven heads were at an early stage identified with Roman emperors, and the expected eighth head (Revelation 17:11), with a Nero *redivivus*. As for the number 666, it is generally agreed that the author was here using the method of *gematria*, i.e., equating letters of an alphabet with numerals. Using the Hebrew alphabet, one can get Nero out of the puzzle, and this may well be the intended solution, but at a more fundamental level of symbolism, 666 persistently falls short of 7, the number of completeness, and parodies 888, the perfect number of Jesus; 666 is also 'triangular,' in contrast to the 'square' of the elect – 144,000 – and of the New Jerusalem (see Revelation 7:4; 21:16).

A typical early medieval interpretation of the dragon and the beasts is that of Beatus of Liebana (8th century). All these figures, he argues, are limbs of Antichrist. The seven heads and ten horns symbolized Roman emperors, but they also, by extension, suggest all evil political powers. Nero, in particular, prefigures Antichrist, who now reigns secretly but will someday be manifest (*In Apocalypsim Libri Duodecim*, ed. H.A. Sanders, 1930, 23, 133, 456–98). Although Beatus wrote in Spain under the scourge of Islamic invasions, he did not specifically identify Mahomet or the Saracens with one of these symbols of evil. In the next century, however, Alvarus of Cordoba saw Mahomet as the precursor of Antichrist and calculated the date of his death as 666 (*Patrologia Latina*, 121.535). Much later Pope Innocent III again equated Mahomet with the number of the beast (*Patrologia Latina*, 216.818), as did Alexander of Bremen in the 13th century in his *Expositio in Apocalypsim*.

A new stimulus to the interpretation of the apocalyptic beasts in historical terms was given by Joachim of Fiore in the later 12th century. He identified the heads of the dragon as the seven chief tyrants persecuting the Church from its beginning: Herod; Nero; Cosdroe, King of Persia (representing Mahomet); Constantius Arrianus; Melsemutus (a Saracen tyrant) or sometimes the Emperor Henry IV; Saladin, a contemporary of Joachim; and the Antichrist still to come. By this pattern he accounted for the seven heads of the beast from the sea and for the scarlet beast of chapter 17. But he also interpreted the beast from the sea as the menace of the Saracens and the beast from the land as a pseudo-pope, the two being prefigured in Nero and Simon Magus. Joachim drew a dragon figure and labelled its heads. This drawing may well have been in front of them when at Messina in 1190–91 Richard Coeur de Lion and his courtiers eagerly discussed Antichrist and the dragon with Joachim himself. This figure was circulated, imitated, and discussed in the following century – for example, by the Franciscans Thomas of Pavia and Salimbene di Adam.

Joachim set the medieval precedent for a radical reinterpretation of the conflict with the forces of evil. In the pseudo-Joachimist works of the 13th century, the sixth or seventh head of the dragon was identified with the Hohenstaufen Emperor Frederick II or one of his brood, and later the expected political tyrant was variously interpreted as a contemporary ruler. Joachim's interpretation that the beast from the land would be a false religious Antichrist – an idea derived directly from the Apocalypse – was seized upon and developed into a programme in which false pope and political tyrant combined their evil forces against the Church. This view characterized several of the radical Franciscans, including Peter John of Olivi. Ubertino da Casale in the early 14th century actually identified the two beasts as Popes Boniface VIII and Benedict XI, whose 'number' he read as 666, and although such an extreme interpretation was rare at that time, the idea of a pseudo-pope personifying one of the limbs of Antichrist became widespread even among orthodox commentators. An echo of this radical interpretation can be seen in Dante's use of the seven-headed monstrosity and the whore in *Purgatorio*, 32, and it became part of antipapal rhetoric in the era of the Great Schism (1378–1417), for English tradition most notably in the later writings of John Wyclif and the Lollards.

When after the fall of Constantinople in 1453 western Europe was shocked into awareness of the Turkish threat, the dragon figure returned with an Eastern face to haunt the imagination. William Aytinger, reviving in 1498 a timely edition of the so-called *Revelations of Methodius*, drew a lurid picture of the beast from the sea as the total force of Mahomet, including the seven kingdoms of the Turks and their ten provinces (chapter 2). These supposed revelations went into a number of editions.

For Protestants the powers of the dragon were focused in the papacy at Rome. An early Protestant commentator on the Apocalypse, Francis Lambert (*Exegesis in Sanctam Divi Ioannis Apocalypsim Libri VII*, 1539, 416–63), first interpreted the seven heads in terms of the whole of history and then as the persecutors of the true Church: (1) Jews; (2) idolaters; (3) heretics; (4) hypocritical churchmen and Mahomet; (5) false sects; (6) the abomination in the papacy and the Mohammedan menace again; and (7) the Antichrist. To his own generation belonged the sixth tribulation – a tribulation of the two beasts, one from land and one from sea: the papists and the Turks. The Swiss divine. Bullinger, in his *A Hundred Sermons upon the Apocalips of Jesu Christe* (1561), saw the papacy, the beast from the land, as having succeeded the power of the Roman Empire, the beast from the sea. Various Protestant writers fastened on the episode of Joachim and Richard I at Messina. John Foxe, for example, in *Actes and Monuments* (1563) related how Joachim expounded the seven heads down to the final one, Antichrist:

> And this Antichrist (he sayde) was already borne in the citie of Rome, and should be there exalted in the Apostolicall see... And then shall the wicked man be revealed, whom the Lord shall consume with the spirits of his mouth, and shall destroye with the brightnesse of his coming.

Such associations govern the apocalypticism of Spenser in *The Faerie Queene*. From his vision of the New Jerusalem, Redcrosse Knight is imbued with new strength to go forth and slay the Great Dragon (1.9) – a dragon Spenser's audience is clearly expected to associate with the papacy (or even Catholic Spain, the archenemy, threatening to devour the 'woman's issue' of Revelation 12, the new Protestant dynasty).

The whore on the scarlet beast was universally taken by Protestant commentators to represent the pope at Rome. Thus John Napier identified the whore as the 'verie presente City of Rome' and the 'great horned beast' as the 'whole bodie of the Latine Empire, whereof the antichrist is a part' (*A Plaine Discovery of the Whole Revelation of St John*, 1593, 34, 36). Thomas Brightman interpreted the dragon and the first beast as Roman emperors and later the Turks, while the second beast and the whore on the scarlet beast stood for the popes and papal Rome (*A Revelation of the Revelation*, 1615, 552–53, 571–88). The hopes of many expectant prophets in England in the 1640s and 1650s hung on the belief that the dominion of the beast was nearing its end. E. Burroughs, in *A Measure of the Times* (1657), is optimistic:

> And now after the long night of Apostacy and darknesse which hath been upon the face of the earth, is the Lord approaching and his day dawning, and his light breaking

forth as the glory of the morning, and the Kingdome of God is revealed, and his dominion is setting up, after the long reigne of the Beast.

Despite such apparent optimism about the unfolding of apocalyptic events, new and varied interpretations for the dragon-beasts continued to emerge; to the Fifth Monarchists, splitting off from the government in the Barebones Parliament of 1653, Oliver Cromwell looked less like St George than like the 'little horn' or the dragon himself. In Milton's *Reason of Church Government urg'd against Prelaty* (1642) the Anglican prelates are associated with the dragon, the Presbyterians in Parliament with 'our old patron St George'. In *Paradise Lost* Milton allots the final victory, however, not to Michael the archangel or to St George but (on the authority of Revelation 12:11) to the Son of God himself.

Writers in the 18th century seem in general to have lost interest in the dragon of the Apocalypse. Even Blake passes over what might have seemed an irresistible opportunity for expansion of his repertoire of apocalyptic symbolism – although his protean serpent occasionally appears where one might expect a dragon. Imagery drawn from the defeat of the dragon by Michael recurs in the 19th century. Coleridge in his sonnet to Sheridan laments 'the apostate by the brainless rout adored, / As erst the elder Fiend beneath great Michael's sword'. And George Eliot in *The Spanish Gypsy* speaks of ridding the earth – much in the manner of Michael – of 'human fiends / who carry hell for pattern in their souls':

> The great avenging angel does not crawl
> To kill the serpent with mimic fang;
> He stands erect, with sword of keenest edge
> That slays like lightning.

In the 20th century, various versions of the apocalyptic dragon persist in science fiction and fantasy literature. Notable examples in which the biblical associations are apparent are J.R.R. Tolkien's *The Lord of the Rings* and W.H. Reddy's *The Worm Ourobouros*.

Marjorie Reeves
St Anne's College, Oxford University

Last Judgment

Warnings of God's judgment on the wickedness of Israel and Israel's enemies abound in the Old Testament and are particularly developed in the prophetic descriptions of the Day of the Lord (Amos 1:2 – 6:14) and the vengeance of God (Nahum 1:2–8). In general this judgment is collective, on the nation or on all sinners, and does not necessarily result in the end of human history. A destruction of the world, symbolized by the universal flood (Genesis 7) and the rain of fire on Sodom and Gomorrah (Genesis 19), is threatened in the later prophets and in apocalyptic works (Daniel 2:31–45), as well as in the New Testament, which compares the evil of the last days with the time of Noah (Matthew 24:37). These later writings also conceive of judgment as individual, on each person 'according to his works' (Ezekiel 7:8) and revealing 'the secrets of the heart' (Romans 2:16), a judgment from which the evil will try to hide by calling mountains upon their heads (Revelation 6:16). The judge will be the Ancient of Days, whose assessor is the Son of man (Daniel 7:9–13), a figure which the New Testament associates with Jesus Christ (Matthew 24:30).

Preceded by signs and wonders (Joel 2:30–32; Matthew 24:29–30; Revelation 6:12–14), the release of Gog and Magog (Revelation 20:8), the battle of Armageddon (Revelation 16:16), the resurrection of the dead (Isaiah 26:19; Daniel 12:2; Revelation 11:11), and the second coming of Christ (Revelation 1:7), the time of judgment is known only to God the Father (Matthew 24:36) and will surprise many as a thief in the night (Matthew 24:43). At the blast of a trumpet (Isaiah 27:13; Matthew 24:31; Revelation 11:15), Jesus Christ will send his angels to gather mankind at the great white throne (Revelation 20:11–15). For the evildoers it will be worse than it was for Sodom and Gomorrah (Matthew 10:15), resulting in a fate of everlasting fire amid weeping and wailing and gnashing of teeth (Matthew 24:51). In the presence of the archangel Michael (Daniel 12:1), and reading from the opened books, God will judge each individual, meting out justice measure for measure (Isaiah 27:8) by rewarding the righteous with eternal life in the New Jerusalem (Revelation 21) and damning those whose names are not found in the book of life (Revelation 20:15) to fire and brimstone (Revelation 21:8).

Sinful creation will be destroyed and replaced by a new heaven and new earth (Revelation 21:1).

Portrayals of the Last Judgment in medieval art and literature emphasize the wretchedness of mankind when beyond mercy and facing a wrathful and strict judge. Even the saved are stricken by terror under his scrutiny. Other works which do not explicitly describe the Last Judgment nevertheless allude to this central eschatological expectation in establishing the significance of the actions they portray. For example, at the conclusion of *The Canterbury Tales*, the Parson calls the pilgrims to contrition by reminding them of the certainty of Doomsday. Chaucer thus juxtaposes the end of the pilgrimage with suggestions of a final judgment at the end of life and the world. In *Cleanness* the *Pearl* Poet concentrates on commonplace typology of judgment, describing, for example, the universal Deluge and the destruction of Sodom to prefigure the terrible wrath of God and final punishment of evil.

The Last Judgment is especially prominent in early drama. In the Chester cycle 'Prophets of Antichrist,' Old Testament and New Testament prophets prophesy the general resurrection, Antichrist, the Fifteen Signs of Doomsday, and Judgment Day. Since they treat the entire course of salvation history from creation to the end of the world, all four major Middle English mystery cycles conclude with a 'Last Judgment'. Although sharing in common the basic doctrinal features outlined in Christian eschatology, including Christ's condemnation of the wicked, the cycle plays vary remarkably in developing their dramatic possibilities, so that the effect of the Last Judgment plays ranges from the highly formal pageantry of the Chester cycle to the comic escapades of Tutivillus in the Towneley cycle. Universal judgment is less prominent in the morality plays since they deal with the experience of the individual rather than with salvation history. Nevertheless, the 'Castle of Perseverance' dramatizes the Four Daughters of God debating the relative demands of mercy and justice in judgment, with Peace concluding:

> We schal devoutly pray
> At dredful domysday,
> And I schal for us say
> That Mankind schal have grace. (3544–47)

The play ends at the judgment throne. The Bad Angel is sent to hell, Mankind is welcomed to the right hand of God, and the audience is warned that 'Whanne Mihel his horn blowith at my dred dom' a reckoning will be demanded 'At my gret jugement' (3617–22).

Renaissance drama does not stage the Last Judgment, although in Marlowe's *Doctor Faustus* Faustus, nearing the end of this life, calls on 'Mountaines and hilles, come, come, and fall on me, / And hide me from the heavy wrath of God' (1436–39; cf. Revelation 6:15–16). Several other Renaissance plays, including Shakespeare's *Measure for Measure* and Tourneur's *The Atheist's Tragedy*, develop patterns common in earlier dramatic treatments of doomsday.

In Robert Herrick's 'In the Hour of My Distress,' allusions to Doomsday support petitions for mercy or divine comfort at the time 'When the Judgment is revealed, / And that opened which was sealed'. In some instances 'Doomsday' is used as a word of shorthand to signify the end of history, as when Macbeth, reacting to the phantasmagoric eight kings produced by the witches, asks, 'What, will the line stretch out to th' crack of doom?' (*Macbeth*, 4.1.117). Milton refers to the coming of Christ in judgment as a gift of the Father (*De Doctrina Christiana*, 1.5). Longer descriptions of Judgment Day are less frequent. They include the divine prophecy of the Last Judgment in *Paradise Lost* (3.323–43) and two short yet powerful poems by George Herbert: 'Doomsday,' which concentrates on the Resurrection and creates an overwhelming sense of urgency; and 'Judgment,' which notes the despair of 'poore wretches' and calls on Christ's promises to argue that 'my faults are thine'.

More recent poets have both amplified and transformed the literary treatment of the Last Judgment. Pope composes an extravagant parody in book 4 of *The Dunciad*, a judgment enacted by the Goddess Dulness as she seeks to establish a new kingdom of Dull on earth (the object of Pope's poem is a satiric attack on contemporary poets of whom he disapproved; cf. Byron's *Vision of Judgment*, which uses apocalyptic imagery in satirizing the poetry of Southey). Most self-consciously idiosyncratic is Blake, who, commenting on his 'A Vision of the Last Judgment,' explains that the Last Judgment is 'when all those are Cast away who trouble Religion with Questions concerning Good & Evil'. Throughout his poetry

Blake interfuses traditional expectations with his own prophetic visions. In *Milton* he beholds 'the Twenty-four Cities of Albion / Arise upon their Thrones to Judge the Nations of the Earth' (42.16–17). *The Four Zoas*, Night 9, visualizes the Last Judgment in what Harold Bloom has called 'Blake's most exuberant and inventive poetry' (*Blake's Apocalypse*, 266). The dream concludes with a new peace: 'The war of swords departed now / The dark Religions are departed & sweet Science reigns' (139.9–10).

Other noteworthy reworkings of this eschatological theme include Browning's 'Easter Day' (546–734), which is conceived as an intense inner dialogue on Judgment Day describing Christ the Judge in awful majesty; William Lisle Bowles' *St John in Patmos* (3.228–63), which explicates the prophet's vision of the end; and James Westfall Thompson's *The Lost Oracles*, a masque which in its fourth act stages a Last Judgment.

Richard K. Emmerson
Western Washington University

Laodicea

In the Revelation of St John the aged disciple of Jesus hears the Spirit pronounce judgment upon the 'seven churches which are in Asia'. One of these is 'the church of the Laodiceans', unto whom John is to write the Spirit's words: 'I know thy works, that thou art neither cold nor hot: I would thou wert cold or hot. So then because thou art lukewarm, and neither cold nor hot, I will spew thee out of my mouth' (Revelation 3:14–16).

In John Bunyan's *Grace Abounding*, the narrator reports how the Tempter tried to discourage him from perseverance by saying, 'You are very hot for mercy, but I will always cool you; this frame [of mind] shall not last always: Many have been as hot as you... but I have quenched their zeal... I will cool you insensibly, by degrees, by little and little.' Thomas Hardy, raised in the precincts of such a warning, writes of Gabriel in *Far from the Madding Crowd* that 'On Sundays he was... one who felt himself to occupy morally that vast middle space of Laodicean neutrality which lay between the Communion people of the parish and the drunken section' (chapter 1); Manston of *Desperate*

Remedies is similarly said to be 'Laodicean' of religion. (Hardy's *A Laodicean*, 1881, borrows from a theologian's article on Revelation 3:14–16, that of Charles Apperly in the 1833 *Quarterly Review*.) Sinclair Lewis' preacher turns a familiar term against his hearers when he cants, 'Oh, woe to the Congregationalists for that you are all weak, wabbly, halfway-covenanting Laodiceans' (*The God-Seeker*, chapter 15). An ancient vice is sometimes heralded as a modern virtue: Ernest, in Samuel Butler's *The Way of All Flesh*, writes an essay in which he argues that a modern person should not 'feel very strongly upon any subject... We should be... somewhat lukewarm churchmen... The Church herself should approach as nearly to that of Laodicea as was compatible with her continuing to be a Church at all, and each individual member should only be hot in striving to be as lukewarm as possible'. G.B. Shaw comments: 'Thus the world is kept sane less by the saints than by the vast mass of the indifferent, who neither act nor react in the matter. Butler's preaching of the gospel of Laodicea was a piece of common sense founded on his observation of this' (*Back to Methuselah*, preface).

David L. Jeffrey
University of Ottawa

Marriage Feast

One of the most memorable and influential images of the book of Revelation is the apocalyptic banquet which celebrates the marriage of Christ (here figured as the Lamb) and his bride (the Church, the heavenly city) and inaugurates the new heaven and new earth: 'And he saith unto me, Write, Blessed are they which are called unto the marriage supper of the Lamb' (Revelation 19:9; cf. Revelation 21:2, 9–10; 22:17). The Old Testament background of this image is twofold. The first influence is the persistent metaphor of the covenant as a marriage between God and his people (e.g., Isaiah 54:1–8; 62:4; Ezekiel 16; Hosea 2–6). The second is the notion of a banquet prepared for the redeemed at the end of time.

An apocalyptic banquet for all peoples, held when the Lord has vanquished death, figures in Isaiah 25:6–8, and ritual eating is sometimes associated with the sacrificial slaughter of enemies on the day of triumph (e.g., Ezekiel 39:17–20; Zephaniah 1:7–9). Leviathan, an archetypal enemy, becomes a sacrifice and food for the people in Psalm 74:12–17. A messianic banquet is a commonplace feature of Jewish apocalyptic thought. In Apocalypse of Baruch 29:4–8 Leviathan and Behemoth 'shall be food for all that are left'. A midrash on Psalm 23:5 identifies them as the feast laid out when God 'preparest a table before me in the presence of mine enemies'. According to Ethiopic Enoch 62:14, the righteous shall eat with the son of man. The Apocalypse of Elijah tells of a forty-year interregnum with supernatural abundance of food which the righteous eat with the Messiah.

In the New Testament the marriage supper figures as a general motif both in the parables of the marriage feast (Matthew 22:1–14; Luke 14:15–24) and of the wise and foolish virgins (Matthew 25:1–13) and in the recurrent narratives of miraculous feeding. Jesus refers both to himself as the bridegroom and to celebratory feasting in the Gospels (Matthew 9:15; Mark 2:19–20; Luke 5:34–35; cf. John 3:29), and alludes to an apocalyptic banquet at which 'Many shall come from the east and west and shall sit down with Abraham, and Isaac, and Jacob, at the feast in the kingdom of heaven' (Matthew 8:11; cf. Luke 14:15). Those who have proven faithful can expect to dine at Jesus' table with him as the host (Luke 22:28–30). The apocalyptic banquet is also explicitly anticipated by the last supper of Christ, and commemorated in the Eucharist (1 Corinthians 11:23–26).

'Blessed are they which are called unto the marriage supper of the Lamb' (Revelation 19:9) subsumes all earlier biblical marriage-feast imagery in a vision of a people redeemed through a symbolic marriage to the true king, at which they are both guests and marriage partner. (The promise in Revelation 2:7 suggests the persecuted and martyrs as special participants.) This apocalyptic marriage requires the annihilation of the bride's demonic parody, the scarlet whore of Babylon, symbolic of all tyrannies, physical and spiritual, from which redemption is needed (as in Revelation 17–18).

Herbert's 'Love (3),' with evident reference to Jesus' parable of the wedding feast (Luke 14:15–24), pictures a banquet to which 'Love bade me welcome'. The speaker, guilt-ridden, protests his unworthiness but is ultimately compelled by love to 'sit and eat'.

Vaughan's 'The Feast' deals principally with the sacramental communion of the Lamb 'in the next world'; by comparison, to 'toil and sow, / That wealth may flow' in this world is to pursue unreality. Milton's dead Lycidas 'hears the unexpressive nuptial Song, / In the blest Kingdoms meek of joy and love' (176–77), while his Damon, who 'did not taste the delight of the marriage bed,... shall enact [his] part eternally in the immortal marriage where song and the sound of the lyre are mingled in ecstasy with blessed dances, and where the festal orgies rage under the heavenly thyrsus' ('Epitaphium Damonis', 214–19; translated by Bush).

In Blake's *Milton* 'the supper of the Lamb & his bride' features centrally in Los' grand vision of the awakening of Albion. Coleridge's *Rime of the Ancient Mariner* begins with the Mariner detaining one of three guests bidden to a wedding feast. Although protesting that the 'Bridegroom's doors are opened wide' and that he is not only invited but obligated to attend, the Wedding Guest nonetheless stays to hear the tale and to be instructed in the meaning of love and communion. In Emily Dickinson's 'There came a day...' a friendship (about to suffer separation) is a rehearsal 'Lest we too awkward show / At Supper of the Lamb'. E.J. Pratt, in 'The Depression Ends,' speaks of using the magic of Prospero to 'usher in the golden era / With an apocalyptic dinner'.

Richard Schell
Laurentian University

Michael

Michael, usually listed as first of the archangels, appears to Daniel in a vision as 'one of the chief princes' (Daniel 10:13), by implication a kind of special guardian angel to Israel (10:21) who shall again come to Israel's aid in the last days, in the time of the Great Tribulation (12:1; cf. Revelation 12:7–9). His name is said to mean 'Who is like God?' according to some targums (e.g., Targum Yerushalmi, Numbers 2:10) from utterances to that effect made at the crossing of the Red Sea and the handing down of the Torah to Moses, and talmudic legend makes him one of the four archangels who stand around the throne of God in heaven (the others being Gabriel, Uriel, and

Raphael). In some sources he succeeds Shammiel (or Sammael) as leader of the heavenly choir following the excommunication of Lucifer and his cohorts (Seder Rabba di-Bereshit 28–30; 3 Hekalot 161–63; Genesis Rabba 78.2); he is sometimes given the name Metatron, and said to be the angel who wrestled with Jacob at the Jabbok (Abkir in Yalqut 1.132; Zerubbabel 5.5), from which event he had to return before daybreak so as to lead the choir in morning song (Genesis Rabba 78.1–2; Tannaim Bereshit 1.165). The appearance of Michael, and sometimes of Gabriel, was thought to indicate the presence of the Shekinah (Genesis Rabba 97.3; cf. Justin, *Dial*, 20, 128), and he is associated by various sources with the ascension of Enoch and Moses. In a rarer midrash the seraph which touched Isaiah's lips with a live coal is identified as Michael (Berakot 4b). The New Testament Epistle of Jude (v. 9) recollects a talmudic legend that Michael preserved the body of Moses from Sammael, the devil who had claimed it on account of Moses having murdered the Egyptian (cf. 2 Petirat Mosheh 381–82; Midrash D'varim Raba 11.10; also Origen, *On First Principles*, 3.2.1).

Michael's role in Daniel 12:1 and Revelation 12:7–9 largely defines his role in medieval Christian commentary and legend, where he becomes the angel who rescues souls from Limbo and Hell. In representations of the Last Judgment he is shown armed as a warrior, holding the scales which balance good deeds against bad (Picinelli, *Mundus Symbolicus*).

In Milton's *Paradise Lost* Michael and Gabriel lead the war in heaven against Satan, where he is called by God 'of Celestial Armies Prince' (6.44). It is something of a comedown when Byron in his 'Vision of Judgment' has Michael receive the soul of King George III into heaven, and thus illustrates his point:

> 'Twas the archangel Michael; all men know
> The make of angels and archangels, since
> There's scarce a scribbler has not one to show,
> From the fiends' leader to the angels' prince. (stanza 29)

In Joyce's *Portrait of the Artist*, there is a reference to 'Michael, prince of the heavenly host,' who 'with a sword of flame in his hand, appeared before the guilty pair [Adam and Eve] and drove them forth [from Eden],' drawing upon a tradition reflected in book 10 of Milton's *Paradise Lost*, in which also is found reference to the expectation that it will be Michael who blows the trumpet in the last day, announcing the Final Judgment (10.73–75).

David L. Jeffrey
University of Ottawa

Millennium

The idea of the millennium (the thousand years during which Satan will be bound) may depend upon an interpretation of the days of Creation as forecasting a cosmic World Week of history in which each day represents one thousand years (see, e.g., Pseudo-Philo 28.8–9; Slavonic Enoch 33). This scheme culminates in the seventh, the Sabbath Age, a concept which became assimilated to the Jewish prophetic hope of a messianic kingdom in this world. The earthly character of this blessed age originated in a time when Jews did not expect an afterlife. When in later thought a state beyond time was expected, Jewish commentators interpreted the millennium as an intermediate reign of fruitfulness and peace upon earth before the conclusion of history (4 Ezra 7:28–35).

In the New Testament no writer explicitly took up the theme of the millennium except the author of the Apocalypse. The way he depicts it implies an earthly messianic regime which will have a definite end when Satan is loosed for a little while. He is here following Jewish tradition: the millennium will be Christ's reign on earth as God's Messiah. As G.B. Caird writes: 'John wants the best of both worlds: the ultimate destiny of the redeemed is in the heavenly city, but he retains the earthly paradise, the millennium... God has a purpose for the whole Creation and his purpose must be vindicated in history' (*A Commentary on the Revelation of St John the Divine*, 254).

St John's use of the Jewish millennium opened the door to Christian expectations of a blessed future age. Papias (early 2nd century), whose vision of an era of prodigious natural fecundity also shows Jewish influence, was followed by St Irenaeus (late 2nd century), Tertullian and Commodian (3rd century), and Lactantius (4th century), who expected a glorious reign of Christ and his saints for a thousand years on earth. But the dangers of millenarianism (Greek, chiliasm) were soon apparent to some, at least, of the early Church Fathers. Tyconius (late 4th century) supplies an alternative interpretation, that the thousand years means the spiritual victory of Christ which extends from the First to the Second Advent. St Jerome rejects a literal millennium as mere fable, while his contemporary St Augustine, although at first attracted by the idea, later dismisses it as ridiculous. From the 5th century onwards literal millennial dreams would seem to have been stamped out by the weight of such authoritative exegesis.

But the idea continued to haunt a troubled and war-ridden Europe. Thus the crusading movement was in part the pursuit of a millennium focused on the earthly Jerusalem which, to the poor who flocked in such numbers to the 'People's Crusade' in 1095, appeared as the dream city 'flowing with milk and honey'. A fresh impetus to such expectation was given by Joachim of Fiore (12th century), who supplied a Trinitarian basis to this hope by assimilating the idea of the Sabbath Age of history to his concept of the third 'age' of the Holy Spirit. This future third age would follow the main victory over the forces of Antichrist but, because this would still be an age within history, Satan would be loosed at its end and the final scourge of Gog and Magog would immediately precede the conclusion of history at the Last Judgment.

The belief in a Sabbath Age of history, or Millennium, or Age of the Spirit, can be traced through a number of medieval and Renaissance commentaries on the Apocalypse. It inspired the 15th-century sect of the Taborites in Bohemia, who established their communist society on the mountain they called Mt Tabor. A strong defence of millenarianism in a Renaissance context was made by the Dominican Giovanni Annio of Viterbo in a work written in 1481 which proclaimed his belief that a future pope and prince would together destroy the Saracens, unite all Christians, and inaugurate a final state of beatitude in the Church. Again, at the end of the century, the prophetic vision of Savonarola and his disciples designated Florence as the New Jerusalem. An early 17th-century commentator on the Apocalypse, Bartholomew Holzhauser, places against a black background of present wars and calamities a coming millennium when emperor and pope would break the Turkish power and give peace and justice to the world (*Interpretatio in Apocalypsim*, 1850, 69–75). In the same period certain Franciscan and Jesuit visionaries were focusing their millennial dreams on missions in the New World.

It would seem natural for Protestants to be tempted into a heady millenarianism. By no means all were. For example, Henry Bullinger, the influential pastor of Zurich, in his *A Hundred Sermons upon the Apocalips of Jesu Christe*, 1561, 593–99), writes expressly against the heresy of 'the Chiliastes or Millenaries,' interpreting the thousand years as from the beginning of the gospel preaching to the mid-11th century, the point at which Bullinger saw the papacy as entering upon its most fully satanic course.

There was, however, a strong current of millennial expectation flowing among radical Protestants on the continent, and equivalent aspirations were evident in England. John Bale's play *A comedy concerning three laws* (circa 1531) elaborates the usual seven ages of world history, after the various infidelities of which will come a new heaven of renewed faith and a new earth of faith's practical application. John Foxe, author of the famous *Book of Martyrs* (1563), wrote a commentary on the Apocalypse in which the seven ages are successive millennia, the first six of which are to give way to the final millennial kingdom sometime before AD2000 (*Eicasmi seu Meditationes in Sacram Apocalypsin*, 1587, 60). Sir Walter Raleigh's *History of the World* describes three great periods of world history, before the law, under the law, and under grace (2.4.11). While the last era begins with the birth of Christ, it contains within it 'the promise of an everlasting kingdom'. Raleigh may have been influenced by Robert Pont's *A newe treatise of the right reckoning of the yeares, and ages of the world*; Pont, however, reckons the penultimate age from 1056 to an imminent date, circa 1600, at which point the millennium will begin. Thomas Brightman's chronology reiterates his belief in a period when Christ will reign with his saints on earth, as distinct from in heaven (*A Revelation of the Revelation*, 1615, Pref., 121–22, 199, 256, 559, 851–73). The greatest outburst of millennial expectations occurred in the Civil War and Commonwealth period when radical thinkers saw the political revolution as the prelude to the descent of the New Jerusalem to earth. At that time Christ's saints would be raised in a 'first resurrection' (which they distinguished from the general resurrection at the end of time) and the whole world would be converted and brought under Christ's rule.

Milton's angel Michael in *Paradise Lost* (1.2585–87) prophesies to fallen Adam a millennial restoration and more,

> ...for then the Earth
> Shall all be Paradise, far happier place
> Than this of Eden, and far happier days.

Milton was familiar with Reformation millenarian controversy through his tutor at Christ's College, Joseph Mede. Both in his essays 'Of Reformation' (1641) and 'Animadversions' (1642), influenced by Tyndale, Foxe, Brightman, and Mede, Milton sees his task in part as a preparation of English Puritans for the approaching millennium. He believed that England would be the seat of Christ's millennial empire ('Of Reformation,' in *Works*, 1.525, 614) – unlike Foxe and Bale, who had explicitly denied that God had elected one nation above another, or that a reformed England would prove either a Utopia or a millennial kingdom.

Other millenarian thinkers, however, subscribed, like Milton, to nationalistic chiliasm. Gerrard Winstanley (1648), a radical Puritan, argued that the English Puritan Revolution itself marked the onset of the millennium, and if the revolutionary spirit of the 1790s failed to follow the Puritan eschatological schema, many were happy to extend millennial expectation to national prophecy. Blake's preface to *Milton* yields up the now famous lines ('And did those Feet'), set to music by Sir C.H.H. Parry (1916), a 'working class' hymn envisioning the millennium brought on by social progress – a major theme in 19th-century literature. Blake's *Europe: A Prophecy* (1794), like Coleridge's 'Religious Musings' of the same year, are modelled on Milton's 'On the Morning of Christ's Nativity,' except that each undertakes to adapt Milton's celebration of the First and Second Advent of Christ to contemporary revolution and its expected consequences, a 'renovated Earth,' a communist utopia in which, in Coleridge's phrase, 'the vast family of Love / Raised from the common earth by common toil / Enjoy the equal produce' (340–43; cf. 356–66).

M.H. Abrams has shown that 'at the formative period of their lives, major romantic poets' (including Wordsworth, Blake, Southey, Coleridge, and Shelley) shared a 'hope in the French Revolution as the portent of universal felicity' (*Natural Supernaturalism*, 64), anticipating in this way the post-Marxian idealists of the next century, from Romantic medievalists like William Morris to Fabian socialists such as G.B. Shaw. After the French Revolution proved not, after all, to usher in a glorious, peaceable kingdom, some of the Romantics tended, like Wordsworth in his Prospectus, to shift their millennial aspirations to a perfection of the powers of human consciousness. Byron's several allusions to the millennium (especially Revelation 20:1–3) also imply such a secularized understanding (e.g., *Don Juan*, 8.1081–84; *Marino Faliero*, 4.2.504–05; *The Prophecy of Dante*, 3.9–12).

In America, the development of literary references to the biblical millennium ran a slightly different course. Here nationalistic chiliasm was the dominant mode for more than two centuries, and it is reflected in a wide range of Puritan and later literature. In a sermon to passengers of the *Arabella* in 1630, John Cotton proclaimed America as the new promised land, reserved by God for his elect people as the actual site for a new heaven and a new earth. John Winthrop's *A Model of Christian Charity*, likewise a sermon delivered on the deck of the flagship *Arabella*, sees all history converging upon the new settlement. Though afflictions were to be endured, for Increase Mather, 'This is Immanuels Land. Christ by a wonderful Providence hath dispossessed Satan, who reigned securely in these Ends of the Earth, for Ages the Lord knoweth how many, and here the Lord has caused as it were *New Jerusalem* to come down from Heaven' (*The Day of Trouble Is Near*). In *Magnalia Christi Americana* Cotton Mather claims prophetic vocation as 'Herald of the Lord's Kingdome now approaching,' and through his work on biblical chronology he assures his readers of an imminent 'Sabbatism... just going to lay its arrest upon us'. He views the American pioneer struggle as 'the last conflict with anti-christ' before the millennium begins.

Though far more theocratic than any vision of England after Milton, the American millennial myth nonetheless parallels its trans-Atlantic counterpart to a considerable degree. As Bercovitch suggests of the American Puritans, 'Far from being nostalgic or primitivistic, their paradise was to be the result of a series of reformations in history, and therefore a fulfilment of social as well as spiritual norms' (*American Jeremiad*, 111).

Later, the American Revolution made 1776 the apocalyptic moment (Samuel Sherwood, *The Church's Flight into the Wilderness*, 1776). Timothy Dwight, sometime president of Yale and signer of the Declaration of Independence, reflected on that moment when he wrote, 'This great continent is soon to be filled with the praise and piety of the Millenium; *here*, is the stem of that wonderful tree whose topmost boughs will reach the heavens' (*A Discourse on the National Fast*, 1812). In his epic poem *The Conquest of Canaan*, he reiterates the theme.

These formative works of American literature and spirituality chart a tradition of American millenarianism which includes elements as diverse as the visionary poetry of Walt Whitman and the formation of radical religious communities such as the Millerites and Campbellites. The same tradition informs the literature of Christian socialism and Social Gospelism, a force affecting Canadian as well as American literary uses of the millennial theme.

As even a cursory overview will show, interest in the 'thousand years' of Revelation 20:3 has been immense, controversial, and as curiously applied in the New World as in the Old. The added burden incumbent upon moderns of bringing it about themselves evokes an understandable weariness of the subject in G.K. Chesterton, who quips: 'We are to remove mountains and bring the millennium, because then we can have a quiet moment to discuss whether the millennium is at all desirable' (*Charles Dickens*, chapter 11).

David L. Jeffrey
University of Ottawa
Marjorie Reeves
St Anne's College, Oxford University

River of Life

In Revelation 22:1 the apostle John pictures a 'pure river of the water of life, clear as crystal, proceeding out of the throne of God and of the Lamb'. In the midst of it and on either side is the tree of life with its twelve fruits and healing leaves (Revelation 22:2). The water is freely available to whoever desires it (Revelation 22:17). The Lamb shall lead the martyrs to living fountains (Revelation 7:17). In the Old Testament this river is associated with the Garden of Eden (Genesis 2:10), the Temple on Zion (Ezekiel 47:1–12), and the City of God (Psalm 46:4; Zechariah 14:8); it signifies fertility, rejuvenation, joy, and eternal life, all of which allusions are incorporated into John's vision.

In English literature the most significant treatments occur in *Pearl* (circa 1380) and in Bunyan's *Pilgrim's Progress*, parts 1 (1678) and 2 (1684). The narrator of *Pearl*, having fallen asleep in a garden, finds himself in a brilliant paradise beside a stream gleaming with jewels. On the opposite bank he sees his lost 'pearl', now a Bride of Christ. After instructing him about salvation, she directs him to a hill from which he can view the City, the wounded Lamb, the company of the blessed which includes the Pearl-Maiden, the tree of life, and the clear river, brighter than sun and moon. Despite a warning that death must precede the crossing of the river, the Dreamer attempts to plunge in and his vision abruptly ends. Bunyan's river also represents death, its flavour bitter, its depth varying according to the pilgrim's faith: the mere crossing does not ensure entry into the City. On the near side is Beulah, a *locus amoenus* where the traveller awaits the Master's summons.

Spenser's Redcrosse Knight is saved from the dragon by the silver flood from the well of life (*Faerie Queene*, 1.11.29–30, 46–48). In Milton's *Lycidas*, the drowned hero's apotheosis carries apocalyptic associations of purifying and healing water. The anagogical river appears also in Blake's *Milton* and *Jerusalem* and in Christina Rossetti's *Whitsun Monday* and *Holy City*. It forms part of the Otherworld landscape in such Christian fantasies as George Macdonald's *Lilith* (1895) and C.S. Lewis' *The Last Battle* (1956). Hymnody has popularized the image and its associations with salvation, divine love, grace, fellowship, joy, and release from 'sorrow, sin and death'. Among the most familiar of such hymns are 'O Mother dear, Jerusalem' (1580), John Newton's 'Glorious Things of Thee are Spoken' (1779), the 18th-century Welsh hymn 'Guide Me, O Thou Great Jehovah,' and Robert Lowry's revivalist 'Shall We Gather at the River' (1864).

Muriel Whitaker
University of Alberta

Two Witnesses

According to Christian eschatology, the two witnesses will appear at the end of time as representatives of Christ in the final battle against the powers of evil. Revelation 11:3–13 draws heavily on Old Testament imagery when it describes two prophets dressed in sackcloth and represented by two lamps and two olive trees (cf. Zechariah 4:3) who preach against the beast which ascends from the bottomless pit. They are killed by the beast in the great city called Sodom and Egypt, lie unburied for three and a half days while many rejoice, and then are resurrected by a breath of life from God (cf. Ezekiel 37:10) and taken to heaven. An earthquake then destroys a tenth of the city, killing 7,000, and the seventh trumpet, the Second Advent, follows (Revelation 11:15).

The witnesses are associated with Christ, who in Revelation 1:5 and 3:14 is called a *martys*, or witness, although the context of the passage, which follows the angel's instruction to John that he eat the book (Revelation 10:8–11; cf. Ezekiel 3:1), suggests that the witnesses more generally represent the importance of the prophetic office in the Church in the last days. Their miraculous powers – they use fire against their enemies, prevent rain, turn water into blood, and call forth plagues – also associate them with Elijah (cf. 2 Kings 1:10–15; 1 Kings 17:1) and Moses (Exodus 8–12), both of whom, according to tradition, had been translated to heaven and had appeared together with Christ at the Transfiguration (Mark 9:4–5). The identification of one witness with Elijah is particularly strong, since he had been taken to heaven in a fiery chariot (2 Kings 2:11) and was expected to reappear (Malachi 4:5; Mark 9:11). As early as St Justin Martyr and throughout most of the Middle Ages, however, the second witness was identified with Enoch, the patriarch who 'walked with God' and was taken up to heaven (Genesis 5:22–24). According to medieval exegesis, these two Old Testament figures were held in the earthly paradise, awaiting the appearance of the Antichrist (the beast from the abyss). They were expected to preach against him, convert the Jews to Christianity, and be killed, resurrected, and taken to heaven shortly before Christ's second coming.

In medieval literature, therefore, the two witnesses most

commonly appear in literary treatments of either the earthly paradise or the Antichrist. The major narrative source for their dwelling in the earthly paradise, what the *Parliament of Three Ages* calls 'iles of the Oryent,' is the apocryphal Gospel of Nicodemus. Describing the harrowing of hell, it explains how Adam and the others released by Christ from the confines of Satan interview Enoch and Elijah while passing through the earthly paradise. Brief references to this expectation are common throughout medieval literature, from Old English sermons to the *Cornish Ordinalia's* 'Resurrection'.

The two witnesses have frequently been identified with particular groups, orders, or even individuals within the Church. In the 12th century, Bruno of Segni argued that they represent 'all the doctors of the church'; Joachim of Fiore associated them with two orders of 'spiritual men'; later authors often identified them with the fraternal orders, especially the Franciscans. In Reformation polemics the witnesses were identified by Luther with all those who through the perilous reign of the Antichrist preached the Old Testament and New Testament in opposition to papal doctrine. In his *Christus Triumphans*, John Foxe mentions that Hierologus and Theosebes are imprisoned for opposition to Pseudammus (the papal Antichrist). These characters probably refer both to Latimer and Ridley – who were executed in Oxford – and to the two witnesses, who according to Foxe represent all the Reformers, from Wyclif to Luther, Melanchthon, and Zwingli. Tennyson later takes up the same designation in his 'Sir John Old Castle':

> Burnt – good sir Roger Acton, my dear friend!
> Burnt, too, my faithful preacher, Beverley!
> Lord, give thou power to Thy two witnesses,
> Lest the false faith make merry over them!
> Two – say but thirty-nine have risen and stand,
> Dark with the smoke of human sacrifice,
> Before thy light, and cry continually.

The most important later references to the witnesses are in the works of William Blake, who drew heavily on Revelation for some of his imagery. In 'A Vision of the Last Judgment,' he portrays the two witnesses in a traditional form, as human figures associated with the second coming of Christ who battle against their enemies. His visionary works, however, provide a more dramatic transformation of the tradition. In *Milton*, Blake labels Rintrah and Palamabron as the two witnesses. They are in some ways identified with the biblical witnesses, since Palamabron is associated with codifiers of religion, specifically Moses, and Rintrah is associated with prophets, specifically Elijah. The division in their roles momentarily sets them against each other, but together they 'view the Human Harvest beneath,' and, as in the Apocalypse and throughout tradition, both prepare the universe 'To go forth to the Great Harvest & Vintage of the Nations' (43.1).

Richard K. Emmerson
Western Washington University

War in Heaven

Among the terrible events seen by St John in his Revelation was a 'war in heaven' in which 'Michael and his angels fought against the dragon; and the dragon fought and his angels, And prevailed not; neither was their place found any more in heaven. And the great dragon was cast out, that old serpent, called the Devil, and Satan, which deceiveth the whole world; he was cast out' (Revelation 12:7–9).

A large variety of interpretations attend this passage. Within the English commentary tradition, that of Thomas Brightman, in *A Revelation of the Revelation* (1615), is noteworthy: it takes the passage as predictive of an apocalyptic last battle on earth, in which the Jews would defeat the 'dragon Turk', and the western Protestants defeat the Roman Antichrist (836–38). These temporal forces would be led by 'some excellent man, in whose person he may present a visible Michael' (see also his *A Most Comfortable Exposition of the last and most difficult parts of the Prophecie of Daniel*, 1644, 937). The general outlines of this reading follow from the annotations of Franciscus Junius, incorporated into the 1602 Annotated Geneva New Testament.

Milton applies the motif rather to the rebellion of Lucifer and his cohorts, who are contested by Michael and Gabriel but finally defeated when Christ himself, as champion, throws the rebels out of heaven: 'Nine days they fell; confounded Chaos roared...' (*Paradise Lost*, 1.34–49, 100–105; 6.1–912). In Milton, then, 'War in Heaven / Among th' Angelic Powers' is what sets the stage for the Fall of mankind on earth. In Matthew Henry's *Commentary* the dragon is Satan, while his opponent, figuratively the Woman, is the Church in the world, struggling for victory in Christ: the account is 'not a prediction of things to come, but rather a recapitulation and representation of things past, which, as God would have the apostle to foresee while future, he would have him to review now that they were past, that he might have a more perfect idea of them in his mind' (*Commentary*, 6.1159–60). In Blake's mythic appropriation, 'the apocalypse, like the Incarnation and Crucifixion, must be inseparable from the fallen body' (L. Damrosch, *Symbol and Truth in Blake's Myth*, 1980, 34). The image is therefore redirected: 'This Wine-press is called War on Earth, it is the Printing Press / of Los; and here he lays his words in order above the mortal brain / As cogs are form'd in a wheel' (*Milton*, 29.8–10). Charles Williams' novel *War in Heaven* (1930) is a modern treatment of the Grail legend, in which the Grail is discovered in a country church, then stolen by a black magician, who battles the Archdeacon and a Roman Catholic Duke who attempt to rescue it. Gradually, the quasi-realist narrative becomes a story of titanic apocalyptic struggle between forces of good and evil.

David L. Jeffrey
University of Ottawa

Whore of Babylon

In the course of John's apocalyptic vision, an angel announces that 'Babylon is fallen, is fallen, that great city, because she made all nations drink of the wine of the wrath of her fornication' (Revelation 14:8). Chapters 17 and 18 elaborate: the whore of Babylon sits on many waters (17:1) and on 'a scarlet coloured beast, full of names of blasphemy, having seven heads and ten horns' (17:3); dressed in purple and scarlet, decked with precious jewels and holding a golden cup, she commits fornication with the kings of the earth (17:2 and 4). John marvels at the beast and the woman, whose forehead bears the inscription 'Mystery,' and the angel then offers to explain the symbolism to him (17:6–18). The whore shall be stripped and burned (17:16); the city will collapse (chapter 18). Unfaithful Babylon contrasts with the New Jerusalem, the holy city prepared as a bride for Christ (21:2, 9–10), the woman clothed with the sun (12:1).

The basic image and many of the details found in Revelation derive from the Old Testament prophets, who frequently depict Jerusalem or Israel as an adulteress to the Lord, her true husband. (See Hosea 1–3; Isaiah 1:21; 57:7–13; Jeremiah 3:1–4:4; and especially Ezekiel 16 and 23.) The destruction of Babylon is foretold in Jeremiah 50–51, which draws on Isaiah 3:17–24. Since cultic prostitution was a part of Canaanite religious practice, the metaphor of Judah's hankering after strange gods has particular point. That Babylon is the city or state primarily associated with false and idolatrous belief stems from two considerations. First, the Hebrew name for Babylon, *babel*, recalls the story of the infamous Tower of Babel, destroyed by God as a judgment on the impiety of its builders (Genesis 11). Second, the deportation of the Jews to Babylon, the Babylonian captivity of 604–562BC (2 Kings 24–25), made Babylon the epitome of the kingdom hostile to true religion.

As a city, whorish Babylon is related to other apostate kingdoms, especially Tyre (Isaiah 23:15–18) and Nineveh (Nahum 3:4–6). St Victorinus' *Commentary on the Apocalypse* remarks that the Babylon of Isaiah and Revelation and the Sodom of Ezekiel 'are all one,' and this sort of typological conflation of evil cities influences D.G. Rossetti's 'The Burden of Nineveh,' a poem which alludes to both Rome and Babylon as types of the 'delicate harlot,' Nineveh, before assimilating London to the same scheme. As whore, Babylon is related principally to Jezebel (1 Kings 18:19–19:3), Ahab's queen, who adulterated the faith of Israel (2 Kings 9:1–37). This identification (which Bullinger, e.g., uses in *A Hundred Sermons upon the Apocalypse*, translation 1561) was promoted by Revelation 2:20, which refers to a prophetess named Jezebel who 'seduces my servants to commit fornication'.

Although evidence from the Qumran scrolls has been used to identify the whore of Babylon with unfaithful Jerusalem (*Revelation*, Anchor Bible, 282–88), Rome, the city of seven hills, is usually thought to be figured in the harlot's seven-headed beast (Revelation

17:3). In ancient Judaism it was common to speak of Rome as Babylon *redivivus* (Slavonic Apocalypse of Baruch 11:1; Sibylline Oracles 5:143, 158–59; 4 Ezra 2:36–40; cf. 1 Peter 5:13). This interpretation is confirmed, among the Ante-Nicene Fathers, by Tertullian, St Hippolytus, St Irenaeus, and Victorinus. Although St Augustine neglects the whore of Babylon per se, he adopts the distinction between Jerusalem (peace) and Babylon (confusion) and equates the latter with Rome (*De civitate Dei*, 18.2, 22, 27). Rabanus Maurus says that Babylon is allegorically the church of the Gentiles; anagogically, hell; tropologically, the corrupted soul (*Patrologia Latina*, 112.872). Bishop Haymo argues that Babylon is the house built on sand; Jerusalem the house built on a firm rock (*Patrologia Latina*, 117.1139; cf. Matthew 7:24–27).

In the late medieval prophetic tradition, it was common to see the papacy as the 'ghost of the deceased Roman Empire sitting crowned on the grave thereof' (Hobbes, *Leviathan*, 4.47). In his *Postilla super Apocalipsim*, Peter John of Olivi branded the papacy as the whore because of its cupidity and carnality, and Bernard Gui's *Inquisitor's Manual* (1324) inquires into the errors of the Beguins, a Franciscan order which taught that 'at the end of the sixth era of the Church, the era in which they say we now are, which began with St Francis, the carnal Church, Babylon, the great harlot, shall be rejected by Christ' (McGinn, *Visions of the End*, 219). In England, Wyclif sustains this Franciscan interpretation (*Tractatus de Ecclesia*, 5.356–57). It was the 'Babylonian captivity' of the Avignonese papacy in particular which inspired this denigration, as is seen in Petrarch's sonnet 137, which presents a Babylon dominated by Venus and Bacchus, and in Dante's *Purgatorio*, where the harlot of false religion nestles into the arms of Philip the Fair.

In Reformation polemics, the decrying of the papacy as the whore became ubiquitous and shrill. Luther's way of imagining the Reformation as a release from Babylonian captivity is typical: 'We too were formerly stuck in the behind of this hellish whore, this new church of the pope. We supported it in all earnestness, so that we regret having spent so much time and energy in that vile hole. But God be thanked that he rescued us from the scarlet whore' ('Against Hanswurst'). John Bale contrasts 'the poore persecuted church of

Christ or immaculate spouse of the lamb' with 'the proude paynted churche of the pope, or sinneful Synagogue' and applies this contrast to current affairs by associating Winchester, Bonner, and the 'Romish' bishops with the whore and Cranmer and the Protestants with the pure spouse (*The Image of Bothe Churches*, circa 1548). Bale, like Milton later (in his *Means to Remove Hirelings* and *Of Reformation*), dates the establishment of the meretricious church with the Donation of Constantine, even though that document purporting to give the church temporal power had been exposed as fraudulent during the 15th century. The Geneva Bible's gloss on 2 Thessalonians 2:3–4 links the strumpet with the 'man of sin' (Antichrist) there described, and this link occurs frequently during the 17th century when almost any political power could expect to be traduced in this way. As D.H. Lawrence points out in his idiosyncratic commentary on Revelation, inveighing against the whore has continued to be popular among the evangelically persuaded (*Apocalypse*, 1932, 11–13).

Literary appropriations of Revelation 17–18 and the commentaries on it are many and varied. In *Piers Plowman* (B Version), Langland gives his dreamer a vision of two women, Holy Church and Lady Meed. The daughter of False, Meed is a sinister woman who lives in the pope's palace (2.23) and who is as common 'as a cartway' (3.131). The description of her accoutrements (2.8.18) makes clear that she is understood to be the Whore of Babylon. In Passus 3 and 4, she tries to deceive the King and corrupts the court. The King eventually spurns Meed's blandishments with the help of Reason and Conscience. Although papal corruption is attacked by Langland, the allegory is predominantly moral, not historical.

In book 1 of *The Faerie Queene* Spenser introduces Una and Duessa, who represent true and false religion respectively. Duessa, who wears the triple crown of the papacy, is a 'scarlet whore' (8.29) dressed in the manner described in Revelation (4:29). Duessa's Circean golden cup (Revelation 17:4) contrasts with Fidelia's (8.14.25; 10.13.19), so that there may be, as Waters has proposed, direct satire against the Mass, as in the Mistress Missa tradition. Duessa is stripped of her finery (8.46) in a passage which recalls Revelation 17:16 and Isaiah 47:1, 3, 9 and 12 and 3:17, 24. On the historical plane Una is Elizabeth I, whose motto was *semper eadem* ('always constant'), and Duessa is Mary Stuart. Lucifera, the Queen of Pride, is a female version of Nebuchadnezzar, king of Babylon, who is called Lucifer in Isaiah 14:12. On her chariot drawn by seven bestial sins (1.4), she resembles the whore on her seven-headed dragon. This image is explicit in Dekker's *The Seven Deadly Sins of London*.

In *The Whore of Babylon*, Dekker deals with a political contest between a loose Roman empress, whose triple crown represents Spain, France, and Italy; Titania, the fairy queen, is Elizabeth. In 'Tropicall and shadowed collours,' the 'Drammatical Poem' sets forth thinly disguised traitors such as Edmund Campion and Dr Parry; it climaxes with the defeat of the Armada. An inventive twist is the appearance of the 'Truth, the Daughter of Time' motif, frequently attached elsewhere to Elizabeth:

> *Truth:* Besides I am not gorgious in attire,
> But simple, plain and homely; in mine eyes,
> Doves sit, not Sparrowes; on my modest cheekes,
> No witching smiles doe dwell; vpon my tongue
> No vnchast language lies; my Skins not spotted
> With foule disease, as is that common harlot,
> That baseborne truth, that lies in Babylon. (3.3.6–12)

Like Dekker, Donne uses clothing as a way of differentiating two ecclesiastical polities, but he audaciously complicates the conventional responses. After pondering whether Christ's true spouse is 'richly painted' or 'rob'd and tore' as in England and Germany, he concludes that she is 'most trew, and pleasing to thee, then / When she is embrac'd and open to most men' ('Holy Sonnet 18'). In *Bartholomew Fair* Ben Jonson satirizes Zeal-of-the-Land Busy's puritanical strictures against the Whore and Antichrist.

For Blake, the Whore of Babylon is a major archetype. Albion is captivated not by Jerusalem, but by Vala, the Babylon which symbolizes Moral Virtue, Natural Religion, and Deism. This city-state's name is 'Vala in Eternity: in Time her name is Rahab' (*Jerusalem*, 70.17). As the creator of Voltaire and rationalism (*Milton*, 22.41), Rahab is a whore of Babylon (*Four Zoas*, 8.277–82) who seduces mankind 'to destroy Imagination' (*Jerusalem*, 70.17). After she kills Jesus (*Four Zoas*, 3.341), her foulness is revealed. She is burned, as in Revelation, but from the ashes springs anew the form of Natural Religion (*Four Zoas*, 8.618–20). Her daughter is Tirzah, the Prude, and they weave the Natural, as opposed to the Spiritual Body (*Four Zoas*, 8.201, 220). Since both Rahab and Tirzah are associated with the number three, their product is the 'ninefold darkness' of Urizen (see Frye, *Fearful Symmetry*, 1947, 301). Elsewhere Blake associates Rahab with the covering cherub of Ezekiel 28:13–19, who frustrates mankind's attempt to return to paradise (*Jerusalem*, 89.52–53). In *Blake's Apocalypse* (1963), Bloom comments on the name Blake gives the Whore of Babylon. Blake transforms the redeemed harlot Rahab (Joshua 2), the ancestress of Jesus (Matthew 1:5–6), whom exegetes read as a type of the Church, into a demonic figure. 'For him Rahab is indeed the Church, all the Churches, but she is unceasing in her whoredoms, and no one is to be saved through her. Blake identifies the Rahab of Jericho with the other Rahab of the Old Testament, the sea monster associated with Egypt and Babylon in the Psalms [87:4] and Isaiah [51:9], and therefore a type of Job's Leviathan' (259–60).

Although the other Romantic poets were deeply indebted to Revelation (Abrams, *Natural Supernaturalism*, 1971, 41–46), they treated the Whore of Babylon in relatively conventional ways. In the dramatic fragment *Charles the First*, Shelley has the citizens of London comment on Archbishop Laud, whose 'London will soon be his Rome' (1.58), and on Henrietta Maria, the 'Babylonian woman' and 'Canaanitish Jezebel' (1.62, 69). Similar slurs are cast on the Roman Catholic Lady Castlewood in Thackeray's *Henry Esmond*, and similar antipapism occurs in Byron's *Childe Harold* (1.29). Coleridge, in his *Religious Musings* (320–34), evokes the whore as 'mitred Atheism,' and in a footnote explains that Babylon does not refer to Rome exclusively, but 'to the union of Religion with Power and Wealth, wherever it is found'. In 'Characteristics,' Carlyle stigmatizes advertising as the Whore of Babylon. The *femme fatale* tradition overlays images from Revelation in Christina Rossetti's 'The World-Self-Destruction,' when Babylon the Great appears as a harlot intent upon enmeshing her denizens 'in her wanton hair' and as a Salome-like dancer who 'turns giddy the fixed gazer'.

In Hawthorne's *The Scarlet Letter*, Hester is spoken of as 'a scarlet woman, and a worthy type of her of Babylon'. Yet Hawthorne says that were there a papist among the Puritans, he 'might have seen in this beautiful woman, so picturesque in her attire and mien, and with the infant at her bosom, an object to remind him of the image of Divine Maternity'. Robert Lowell includes a poem on 'The Fall of Babylon' in *Land of Unlikeness*, but his most interesting effort in this vein is in 'As a Plane Tree by the Water,' where the Virgin goes almost unrecognized as 'Our Lady of Babylon' through the streets of a city which is a composite of Babylon, Babel, and Boston. Joyce, though sometimes given to direct allusions to the Whore of Babylon, often subtly confuses the virgin with the whore. In *Ulysses*, in the encounter of Bloom with Gerty MacDowell, the colours of rose and scarlet symbolize Dante's Celestial Rose and the scarlet woman respectively: 'He was eyeing her as a snake eyes its prey. Her woman's instinct told her that she had raised the devil in him and at the thought a burning scarlet swept from throat to brow till the lovely colour of her face became a glorious rose.'

Ronald B. Bond
University of Calgary

Woman Clothed with the Sun

Revelation 12:1–6 describes as a great sign in heaven a woman clothed with the sun, standing on the moon, and wearing a crown of twelve stars. Pregnant and in pain to deliver a son who is destined to rule the nations, she is harassed by a great red dragon. This seven-headed creature awaits to devour the baby, but the baby is snatched away to God, and the woman flees to the desert, where she is nourished for 1,260 days.

Although the astrological language used to describe the woman has led scholars to associate her with a sun goddess and various Near Eastern myths, she is in the biblical context more likely a figure of the righteous community – compare the representation of Israel (Isaiah 66:7–11; Ezekiel 16:8) and the Church (2 Corinthians 11:2; Ephesians 5:23–27; Revelation 21:2) as women. The woman in Revelation is associated with the Lamb (Revelation 19:7–8); together they symbolize the community of the righteous and its messianic deliverer in opposition to the Whore of Babylon (Revelation 17) and the dragon. The sharp birth pangs suggest the persecution of the remnant awaiting its deliverance, a concept important to the Qumran community and developed in the Psalms of Thanksgiving (1QH 3). In Christian tradition exegetes have generally considered the woman to be a symbol of the community of the persecuted faithful, specifically the Christian Ecclesia embattled by the forces of the devil. To many medieval and later Christian commentators, the persecution of the woman became the central image of Revelation, which was understood as a whole to be essentially a prophecy of the trials of the holy Church.

According to R.H. Charles, the disappearance of the Messiah from birth until he is anointed 'was an idea familiar to Judaism, but impossible as a purely Christian concept' (*Revelation*, 308, n. 1). The biblical text makes no allusion either to the woman's virginity or to the child being her firstborn. Nevertheless, because the pregnant, embattled woman is reminiscent of the woman whose seed will destroy the serpent in the Protoevangelium (Genesis 3:15) and because the scene parallels the sign given to Ahaz that a woman will bear a son named Immanuel (Isaiah 7:10–17), exegetes as early as St Irenaeus (*Adversus haereses*, 3.22.7) argued for the association with Mary. Often, as in Paschasius Radbertus (*Commentarii in Matthaei Libri XII*, 2.1) and Thomas à Kempis (*Prayers on the Life of Christ*, 1.2.25), the imagery has been applied both specifically to Mary and generally to Ecclesia. After the Reformation and in contrast to the Protestant emphasis on the ecclesial interpretation, Catholic exegetes identified the cosmically arrayed woman with the Virgin and developed the apocalyptic language to describe her Assumption and role as Queen of Heaven and to symbolize the Immaculate Conception. This imagery informs the work of great Spanish and Italian Baroque painters (such as Murillo) and the introit in the Catholic Mass of the Assumption.

The woman's retreat to the desert was frequently identified with the withdrawal of the embattled Christian soul from the everyday world into contemplation. St Bonaventure develops this imagery in his *Collationes*, where the vision of the woman not only represents 'the splendour of the contemplatives, for they possess the sun, the moon and the stars' (20.28), but is also associated with the Church Militant (22.2) and the Christian soul seeking union with God (22.39). The image of the woman as soul is also important in mystical literature, where, as in the work of Mechthild of Magdeburg (*The Flowing Light of the Godhead*, 1.22), the soul is identified with Mary.

Dante describes the Virgin Mary in *Paradiso* (31.118–29) as a queen who, like the sun, outshines all others. Medieval literature not only specifically identifies the woman with Mary (as, e.g., in the Middle English lyric '*Quia Amore Langueo*') but also more generally associates the woman with the Church and the individual soul. An ecclesial interpretation of the woman seems to lie behind portrayal of Lady Holy Church in Langland's *Piers Plowman*, since she is intended to contrast with Lady Mead, a type of the Whore of Babylon; the woman's association with the soul probably informs the portrait of the maiden in *Pearl*, a 14th-century poem heavily dependent on apocalyptic imagery.

Later English literature associates the woman with the true, spiritual Church, often in contrast with the carnal church. This opposition is reflected in the first book of Spenser's *Faerie Queene*. Una, like the woman, is associated with the lamb and has an ancient royal lineage (1.1.5). Furthermore, her parents' kingdom has been besieged for years by the 'huge great Dragon horrible in sight' (1.7.44), who elsewhere, like the apocalyptic dragon, is associated with Duessa, the harlot false church. Blake expands the traditional interpretation of the woman clothed with the sun, for she represents not only the Christian but also the universal Church, 'composed of the Innocent civilized Heathen & the Uncivilized Savage, who, having not the Law, do by Nature the things contain'd in the Law. This State appears like a Female crown'd with stars, driven into the Wilderness: she has the Moon under her feet' (*Vision of the Last Judgment*, 609–10). Developing the image of the woman harassed by the dragon for polemical purposes in *Examiner*, no. 21, Swift identifies the Dissenters attempting to disestablish the Church of England with the seven-headed dragon attacking the woman, who by implication is given a double identity – the Anglican Church and Queen Anne.

More recently, Robertson Davies develops an interesting fictional allusion to the woman. In *Fifth Business* (2.2), the young hero, who especially enjoys reading Revelation, sees in a sudden flash just before sinking into a coma the woman harassed by the dragon. Although he later realizes that the 'vision' was actually a sculpture representing the Immaculate Conception, he initially takes it to be a salvific omen; his subsequent search for the image dominates his life.

Richard K. Emmerson
Western Washington University

REVELATION

PROLOGUE
Revelation 1:1–3

A revelation of Jesus Christ, which God gave him so that he could tell his servants what is now to take place very soon; he sent his angel to make it known to his servant John, and John has borne witness to the Word of God and to the witness of Jesus Christ, everything that he saw. Blessed is anyone who reads the words of this prophecy, and blessed those who hear them, if they treasure the content, because the Time is near.

Part One

The Letters to the Seven Churches

'I AM THE ALPHA AND THE OMEGA'
Revelation 1:4–20

John, to the seven churches of Asia: grace and peace to you from him who is, who was, and who is to come, from the seven spirits who are before his throne, and from Jesus Christ, the faithful witness, the First-born from the dead, the highest of earthly kings. He loves us and has washed away our sins with his blood, and made us a Kingdom of Priests to serve his God and Father; to him, then, be glory and power for ever and ever. Amen. Look, he is coming on the clouds; everyone will see him, even those who pierced him, and all the races of the earth will mourn over him. Indeed this shall be so. Amen. 'I am the Alpha and the Omega,' says the Lord God, who is, who was, and who is to come, the Almighty.

I, John, your brother and partner in hardships, in the kingdom and in perseverance in Jesus, was on the island of Patmos on account of the Word of God and of witness to Jesus; it was the Lord's Day and I was in ecstasy, and I heard a loud voice behind me, like the sound of a trumpet, saying, 'Write down in a book all that you see, and send it to the seven churches of Ephesus, Smyrna, Pergamum, Thyatira, Sardis, Philadelphia and Laodicea.' I turned round to see who was speaking to me, and when I turned I saw seven golden lamp-stands and, in the middle of them, one like a Son of man, dressed in a long robe tied at the waist with a belt of gold. His head and his hair were white with the whiteness of wool, like snow, his eyes like a burning flame, his feet like burnished bronze when it has been refined in a furnace, and his voice like the sound of the ocean. In his right hand he was holding seven stars, out of his mouth came a sharp sword, double-edged, and his face was like the sun shining with all its force.

When I saw him, I fell at his feet as though dead, but he laid his right hand on me and said, 'Do not be afraid; it is I, the First and the Last; I am the Living One, I was dead and look – I am alive for ever and ever, and I hold the keys of death and of Hades. Now write down all that you see of present happenings and what is still to come. The secret of the seven stars you have seen in my right hand, and of the seven golden lamp-stands, is this: the seven stars are the angels of the seven churches, and the seven lamp-stands are the seven churches themselves.'

THE LETTER TO EPHESUS
Revelation 2:1–7

'Write to the angel of the church in Ephesus and say, "Here is the message of the one who holds the seven stars in his right hand and who lives among the seven golden lamp-stands: I know your activities, your hard work and your perseverance. I know you cannot stand wicked people, and how you put to the test those who were self-styled apostles and found them false. I know too that you have perseverance, and have suffered for my name without growing tired. Nevertheless, I have this complaint to make: you have less love now than formerly. Think where you were before you fell; repent, and behave as you did at first, or else, if you will not repent, I shall come to you and take your lamp-stand from its place. It is in your favour, nevertheless, that you loathe as I do the way the Nicolaitans are behaving. Let anyone who can hear, listen to what the Spirit is saying to the churches: those who prove victorious I will feed from the tree of life set in God's paradise."'

THE LETTER TO SMYRNA
Revelation 2:8–11

'Write to the angel of the church in Smyrna and say, "Here is the message of the First and the Last, who was dead and has come to life again: I know your hardships and your poverty, and – though you are rich – the slander of the people who falsely claim to be Jews but are really members of the synagogue of Satan. Do not be afraid of the sufferings that are coming to you. Look, the devil will send some of you to prison to put you to the test, and you must face hardship for ten days. Even if you have to die, keep faithful, and I will give you the crown of life for your prize. Let anyone who can hear, listen to what the Spirit is saying to the churches: for those who prove victorious will come to no harm from the second death."'

THE LETTER TO PERGAMUM
Revelation 2:12–17

'Write to the angel of the church in Pergamum and say, "Here is the message of the one who has the sharp sword, double-edged: I know where you live, in the place where Satan is enthroned, and that you still hold firmly to my name, and did not disown your faith in me even when my faithful witness, Antipas, was killed among you, where Satan lives.

Nevertheless, I have one or two charges against you: some of you are followers of Balaam, who taught Balak to set a trap for the Israelites so that they committed adultery by eating food that had been sacrificed to idols; and among you too there are some also who follow the teaching of the Nicolaitans. So repent, or I shall soon come to you and attack these people with the sword out of my mouth. Let anyone who can hear, listen to what the Spirit is saying to the churches: to those who prove victorious I will give some hidden manna and a white stone, with a new name written on it, known only to the person who receives it."'

THE LETTER TO THYATIRA
Revelation 2:18–29

'Write to the angel of the church in Thyatira and say, "Here is the message of the Son of God who has eyes like a burning flame and feet like burnished bronze: I know your activities, your love, your faith, your service and your perseverance, and I know how you are still making progress. Nevertheless, I have a complaint to make: you tolerate the woman Jezebel who claims to be a prophetess, and by her teaching she is luring my servants away to commit the adultery of eating food which has been sacrificed to idols. I have given her time to repent but she is not willing to repent of her adulterous life. Look, I am consigning her to a bed of pain, and all her partners in adultery to great hardship, unless they repent of their practices; and I will see that her children die, so that all the churches realize that it is I who test motives and thoughts and repay you as your deeds deserve. But on the rest of you in Thyatira, all of you who have not accepted this teaching or learnt the deep secrets of Satan, as they are called, I am not laying any other burden; but hold on firmly to what you already have until I come. To anyone who proves victorious, and keeps working for me until the end, I will give the authority over the nations which I myself have been given by my Father, to rule them with an iron sceptre and shatter them like so many pots. And I will give such a person the Morning Star. Let anyone who can hear, listen to what the Spirit is saying to the churches."'

THE LETTER TO SARDIS
Revelation 3:1–6

'Write to the angel of the church in Sardis and say, "Here is the message of the one who holds the seven spirits of God and the seven stars: I know about your behaviour: how you are reputed to be alive and yet are dead. Wake up; put some resolve into what little vigour you have left: it is dying fast. So far I have failed to notice anything in your behaviour that my God could possibly call perfect; remember how you first heard the message. Hold on to that. Repent! If you do not wake up, I shall come to you like a thief, and you will have no idea at what hour I shall come upon you. There are a few in Sardis, it is true, who have kept their robes unstained, and they are fit to come with me, dressed in white. Anyone who proves victorious will be dressed, like these, in white robes; I shall not blot that name out of the book of life, but acknowledge it in the presence of my Father and his angels. Let anyone who can hear, listen to what the Spirit is saying to the churches."'

THE LETTER TO PHILADELPHIA
Revelation 3:7–13

'Write to the angel of the church in Philadelphia and say, "Here is the message of the holy and true one who has the key of David, so that when he opens, no one will close, and when he closes, no one will open: I know about your activities. Look, I have opened in front of you a door that no one will be able to close – and I know that though you are not very strong, you have kept my commandments and not disowned my name. Look, I am going to make the synagogue of Satan – those who falsely claim to be Jews, but are liars, because they are no such thing – I will make them come and fall at your feet and recognize that I have loved you. Because you have kept my commandment to persevere, I will keep you safe in the time of trial which is coming for the whole world, to put the people of the world to the test. I am coming soon: hold firmly to what you already have, and let no one take your victor's crown away from you. Anyone who proves victorious I will make into a pillar in the sanctuary of my God, and it will stay there for ever; I will inscribe on it the name of my God and the name of the city of my God, the new Jerusalem which is coming down from my God in heaven, and my own new name as well. Let anyone who can hear, listen to what the Spirit is saying to the churches."'

THE LETTER TO LAODICEA
Revelation 3:14–22

'Write to the angel of the church in Laodicea and say, "Here is the message of the Amen, the trustworthy, the true witness, the Principle of God's creation: I know about your activities: how you are neither cold nor hot. I wish you were one or the other, but since you are neither hot nor cold, but only lukewarm, I will spit you out of my mouth. You say to yourself: I am rich, I have made a fortune and have everything I want, never realizing that you are wretchedly and pitiably poor, and blind and naked too. I warn you, buy from me the gold that has been tested in the fire to make you truly rich, and white robes to clothe you and hide your shameful nakedness, and ointment to put on your eyes to enable you to see. I reprove and train those whom I love: so repent in real earnest. Look, I am standing at the door, knocking. If one of you hears me calling and opens the door, I will come in to share a meal at that person's side. Anyone who proves victorious I will allow to share my throne, just as I have myself overcome and have taken my seat with my Father on his throne. Let anyone who can hear, listen to what the Spirit is saying to the churches."'

Part Two

The Prophetic Visions

A VISION OF HEAVEN
Revelation 4:1 – 5:14

Then, in my vision, I saw a door open in heaven and heard the same voice speaking to me, the voice like a trumpet, saying, 'Come up here: I will show you what is to take place in the future.' With that, I fell into ecstasy and I saw a throne standing in heaven, and the One who was sitting on the throne, and the One sitting there looked like a diamond and a ruby. There was a rainbow encircling the throne, and this looked like an emerald. Round the throne in a circle were twenty-four thrones, and on them twenty-four elders sitting, dressed in white robes with golden crowns on their heads. Flashes of lightning were coming from the throne, and the sound of peals of thunder, and in front of the throne there were seven flaming lamps burning, the seven Spirits of God.

In front of the throne was a sea as transparent as crystal. In the middle of the throne and around it, were four living creatures all studded with eyes, in front and behind. The first living creature was like a lion, the second like a bull, the third living creature had a human face, and the fourth living creature was like a flying eagle. Each of the four living creatures had six wings and was studded with eyes all the way round as well as inside; and day and night they never stopped singing:

> Holy, Holy, Holy
> is the Lord God, the Almighty;
> who was, and is and is to come.

Every time the living creatures glorified and honoured and gave thanks to the One sitting on the throne, who lives for ever and ever,

71

the twenty-four elders prostrated themselves before him to worship the One who lives for ever and ever, and threw down their crowns in front of the throne, saying:

> You are worthy, our Lord and God,
> to receive glory and honour and power,
> for you made the whole universe;
> by your will, when it did not exist, it was created.

I saw that in the right hand of the One sitting on the throne there was a scroll that was written on back and front and was sealed with seven seals. Then I saw a powerful angel who called with a loud voice, 'Who is worthy to open the scroll and break its seals?' But there was no one, in heaven or on the earth or under the earth, who was able to open the scroll and read it. I wept bitterly because nobody could be found to open the scroll and read it, but one of the elders said to me, 'Do not weep. Look, the Lion of the tribe of Judah, the Root of David, has triumphed, and so he will open the scroll and its seven seals.'

Then I saw, in the middle of the throne with its four living creatures and the circle of the elders, a Lamb standing that seemed to have been sacrificed; it had seven horns, and it had seven eyes, which are the seven Spirits that God has sent out over the whole world. The Lamb came forward to take the scroll from the right hand of the One sitting on the throne, and when he took it, the four living creatures prostrated themselves before him and with them the twenty-four elders; each one of them was holding a harp and had a golden bowl full of incense which are the prayers of the saints. They sang a new hymn:

> You are worthy to take the scroll
> and to break its seals,
> because you were sacrificed, and with your blood
> you bought people for God
> of every race, language, people and nation
> and made them a line of kings and priests for God,
> to rule the world.

In my vision, I heard the sound of an immense number of angels gathered round the throne and the living creatures and the elders;

there were ten thousand times ten thousand of them and thousands upon thousands, loudly chanting:

> Worthy is the Lamb that was sacrificed
> to receive power, riches, wisdom,
> strength, honour, glory and blessing.

Then I heard all the living things in creation – everything that lives in heaven, and on earth, and under the earth, and in the sea, crying:

> To the One seated on the throne and to the Lamb,
> be all praise, honour, glory and power,
> for ever and ever.

And the four living creatures said, 'Amen'; and the elders prostrated themselves to worship.

THE SEVEN SEALS
Revelation 6:1 – 8:5

Then, in my vision, I saw the Lamb break one of the seven seals, and I heard one of the four living creatures shout in a voice like thunder, 'Come!' Immediately I saw a white horse appear, and its rider was holding a bow; he was given a victor's crown and he went away, to go from victory to victory.

When he broke the second seal, I heard the second living creature shout, 'Come!' And out came another horse, bright red, and its rider was given this duty: to take away peace from the earth and set people killing each other. He was given a huge sword.

When he broke the third seal, I heard the third living creature shout, 'Come!'

Immediately I saw a black horse appear, and its rider was holding a pair of scales; and I seemed to hear a voice shout from among the four living creatures and say, 'A day's wages for a quart of corn, and a day's wages for three quarts of barley, but do not tamper with the oil or the wine.'

When he broke the fourth seal, I heard the voice of the fourth living creature shout, 'Come!' Immediately I saw another horse appear, deathly pale, and its rider was called Death, and Hades followed at its heels.

They were given authority over a quarter of the earth, to kill by the sword, by famine, by plague and through wild beasts.

When he broke the fifth seal, I saw underneath the altar the souls of all the people who had been killed on account of the Word of God, for witnessing to it. They shouted in a loud voice, 'Holy, true Master, how much longer will you wait before you pass sentence and take vengeance for our death on the inhabitants of the earth?' Each of them was given a white robe, and they were told to be patient a little longer, until the roll was completed of their fellow-servants and brothers who were still to be killed as they had been.

In my vision, when he broke the sixth seal, there was a violent earthquake and the sun went as black as coarse sackcloth; the moon turned red as blood all over, and the stars of the sky fell onto the earth like figs dropping from a fig tree when a high wind shakes it; the sky disappeared like a scroll rolling up and all the mountains and islands were shaken from their places. Then all the kings of the earth, the governors and the commanders, the rich people and the men of influence, the whole population, slaves and citizens, hid in caverns and among the rocks of the mountains. They said to the mountains and the rocks, 'Fall on us and hide us away from the One who sits on the throne and from the retribution of the Lamb. For the Great Day of his retribution has come, and who can face it?'

Next I saw four angels, standing at the four corners of the earth, holding back the four winds of the world to keep them from blowing over the land or the sea or any tree. Then I saw another angel rising where the sun rises, carrying the seal of the living God; he called in a powerful voice to the four angels whose duty was to devastate land and sea, 'Wait before you do any damage on land or at sea or to the trees, until we have put the seal on the foreheads of the servants of our God.' And I heard how many had been sealed: a hundred and forty-four thousand, out of all the tribes of Israel.

From the tribe of Judah, twelve thousand had been sealed; from the tribe of Reuben, twelve thousand; from the tribe of Gad, twelve thousand; from the tribe of Asher, twelve thousand; from the tribe of Naphtali, twelve thousand; from the tribe of Manasseh, twelve thousand; from the tribe of Simeon, twelve thousand; from the tribe of Levi, twelve thousand; from the tribe of Issachar, twelve thousand; from the tribe of Zebulun, twelve thousand; from the tribe of Joseph, twelve thousand; and from the tribe of Benjamin, twelve thousand had been sealed.

After that I saw that there was a huge number, impossible for anyone to count, of people from every nation, race, tribe and language; they were standing in front of the throne and in front of the Lamb, dressed in white robes and holding palms in their hands. They shouted in a loud voice, 'Salvation to our God, who sits on the throne, and to the Lamb!' And all the angels who were standing in a circle round the throne, surrounding the elders and the four living creatures, prostrated themselves before the throne, and touched the ground with their foreheads, worshipping God with these words:

Amen. Praise and glory and wisdom,
thanksgiving and honour and power and strength
to our God for ever and ever. Amen.

One of the elders then spoke and asked me, 'Who are these people, dressed in white robes, and where have they come from?' I answered him, 'You can tell me, sir.' Then he said, 'These are the people who have been through the great trial; they have washed their robes white again in the blood of the Lamb. That is why they are standing in front of God's throne and serving him day and night in his sanctuary; and the One who sits on the throne will spread his tent over them. They will never hunger or thirst again; sun and scorching wind will never plague them, because the Lamb who is at the heart of the throne will be their shepherd and will guide them to springs of living water; and God will wipe away all tears from their eyes.'

The Lamb then broke the seventh seal, and there was silence in heaven for about half an hour.

Next I saw seven trumpets being given to the seven angels who stand in the presence of God. Another angel, who had a golden censer, came and stood at the altar. A large quantity of incense was given to him to offer with the prayers of all the saints on the golden altar that stood in front of the throne; and so from the angel's hand the smoke of the incense went up in the presence of God and with it the prayers of the saints. Then the angel took the censer and filled it from the fire of the altar, which he then hurled down onto the earth; immediately there came peals of thunder and flashes of lightning, and the earth shook.

THE SEVEN TRUMPETS
Revelation 8:6 – 11:19

The seven angels that had the seven trumpets now made ready to sound them. The first blew his trumpet and, with that, hail and fire, mixed with blood, were hurled on the earth: a third of the earth was burnt up, and a third of all trees, and every blade of grass was burnt.

The second angel blew his trumpet, and it was as though a great mountain blazing with fire was hurled into the sea: a third of the sea turned into blood, a third of all the living things in the sea were killed, and a third of all ships were destroyed.

The third angel blew his trumpet, and a huge star fell from the sky, burning like a ball of fire, and it fell on a third of all rivers and on the springs of water; this was the star called Wormwood, and a third of all water turned to wormwood, so that many people died; the water had become so bitter.

The fourth angel blew his trumpet, and a third of the sun and a third of the moon and a third of the stars were blasted, so that the light went out of a third of them and the day lost a third of its illumination, and likewise the night.

In my vision, I heard an eagle, calling aloud as it flew high overhead, 'Disaster, disaster, disaster, on all the people on earth at the sound of the other three trumpets which the three angels have yet to blow!'

Then the fifth angel blew his trumpet, and I saw a star that had fallen from heaven onto the earth, and the angel was given the key to the shaft leading down to the Abyss. When he unlocked the shaft of the Abyss, smoke rose out of the Abyss like the smoke from a huge furnace so that the sun and the sky were darkened by the smoke from the Abyss, and out of the smoke dropped locusts onto the earth: they were given the powers that scorpions have on the earth: they were forbidden to harm any fields or crops or trees and told to attack only those people who were without God's seal on their foreheads. They were not to kill them, but to give them anguish for five months, and the anguish was to be the anguish of a scorpion's sting. When this happens, people will long for death and not find it anywhere; they will want to die and death will evade them.

These locusts looked like horses armoured for battle; they had what looked like gold crowns on their heads, and their faces looked human, and their hair was like women's hair, and teeth like lion's teeth. They had body-armour like iron breastplates, and the noise of their wings sounded like the racket of chariots with many horses charging. Their tails were like scorpions' tails, with stings, and with their tails they were able to torture people for five months. As their leader they had their emperor, the angel of the Abyss, whose name in Hebrew is Abaddon, and in Greek Apollyon.

That was the first of the disasters; there are still two more to come.

The sixth angel blew his trumpet, and I heard a single voice issuing from the four horns of the golden altar in God's presence. It spoke to the sixth angel with the trumpet, and said, 'Release the four angels that are chained up at the great river Euphrates.' These four angels had been ready for this hour of this day of this month of this year, and ready to destroy a third of the human race. I learnt how many there were in their army: twice ten thousand times ten thousand mounted men. In my vision I saw the horses, and the riders with their breastplates of flame colour, hyacinth-blue and sulphur-yellow; the horses had lions' heads, and fire, smoke and sulphur were coming from their mouths. It was by these three plagues, the fire, the smoke and the sulphur coming from their mouths, that the one third of the human race was killed. All the horses' power was in their mouths and their tails: their tails were like snakes, and had heads which inflicted wounds. But the rest of the human race, who escaped death by these plagues, refused either to abandon their own handiwork or to stop worshipping devils, the idols made of gold, silver, bronze, stone and wood that can neither see nor hear nor move. Nor did they give up their murdering, or witchcraft, or fornication or stealing.

Then I saw another powerful angel coming down from heaven, wrapped in cloud, with a rainbow over his head; his face was like the sun, and his legs were pillars of fire. In his hand he had a small scroll, unrolled; he put his right foot in the sea and his left foot on the land and he shouted so loud, it was like a lion roaring. At this, the seven claps of thunder made themselves heard and when the seven thunderclaps had sounded, I was preparing to write, when I heard a voice from heaven say to me, 'Keep the words of the seven thunderclaps secret and do not write them down.' Then the angel that I had seen, standing on the sea and the land, raised his right hand to heaven, and swore by him who lives for ever and ever, and made heaven and all that it contains, and earth and all it contains, and the sea and all it contains, 'The time of waiting is over; at the time when the seventh angel is heard sounding his trumpet, the mystery of God will be fulfilled, just as he announced in the gospel to his servants the prophets.'

Then I heard the voice I had heard from heaven speaking to me again. 'Go', it said, 'and take that open scroll from the hand of the angel standing on sea and land.' I went to the angel and asked him to give me the small scroll, and he said, 'Take it and eat it; it will turn your stomach sour, but it will taste as sweet as honey.' So I took it out of the angel's hand, and I ate it and it tasted sweet as honey, but when I had eaten it my stomach turned sour. Then I was told, 'You are to prophesy again, this time against many different nations and countries and languages and kings.'

Then I was given a long cane like a measuring rod, and I was told, 'Get up and measure God's sanctuary, and the altar, and the people who worship there; but exclude the outer court and do not measure it, because it has been handed over to gentiles – they will trample on the holy city for forty-two months. But I shall send my two witnesses to prophesy for twelve hundred and sixty days, wearing sackcloth. These are the two olive trees and the two lamps in attendance on the Lord of the world. Fire comes from their mouths and consumes their enemies if anyone tries to harm them; and anyone who tries to harm them will certainly be killed in this way. They have the power to lock up the sky so that it does not rain as long as they are prophesying; they have the power to turn water into blood and strike the whole world with any plague as often as they like. When they have completed their witnessing, the beast that comes out of the Abyss is going to make war on them and overcome them and kill them. Their corpses lie in the main street of the great city known by the symbolic names Sodom and Egypt, in which their Lord was crucified. People of every race, tribe, language and nation stare at their corpses, for three-and-a-half days, not letting them be buried, and the people of the world are glad about it and celebrate the event by giving presents to each other, because these two prophets have been a plague to the people of the world.'

After the three-and-a-half days, God breathed life into them and they stood up on their feet, and everybody who saw it happen was terrified; then I heard a loud voice from heaven say to them, 'Come up here,' and while their enemies were watching, they went up to heaven in a cloud. Immediately, there was a violent earthquake, and a tenth of the city collapsed; seven thousand persons were killed in the earthquake, and the survivors, overcome with fear, could only praise the God of heaven.

That was the second of the disasters; the third is to come quickly after it.

Then the seventh angel blew his trumpet, and voices could be heard shouting in heaven, calling, 'The kingdom of the world has become the kingdom of our Lord and his Christ, and he will reign for ever and ever.' The twenty-four elders, enthroned in the presence of God, prostrated themselves and touched the ground with their foreheads worshipping God with these words, 'We give thanks to you, Almighty Lord God, He who is, He who was, for assuming your great power and beginning your reign. The nations were in uproar and now the time has come for your retribution, and for the dead to be judged, and for your servants the prophets, for the saints and for those who fear your name, small and great alike, to be rewarded. The time has come to destroy those who are destroying the earth.'

Then the sanctuary of God in heaven opened, and the ark of the covenant could be seen inside it. Then came flashes of lightning, peals of thunder and an earthquake and violent hail.

WAR IN HEAVEN
Revelation 12:1–12

Now a great sign appeared in heaven: a woman, robed with the sun, standing on the moon, and on her head a crown of twelve stars. She was pregnant, and in labour, crying aloud in the pangs of childbirth. Then a second sign appeared in the sky: there was a huge red dragon with seven heads and ten horns, and each of the seven heads crowned with a coronet. Its tail swept a third of the stars from the sky and hurled them to the ground, and the dragon stopped in front of the woman as she was at the point of giving birth, so that it could eat the child as soon as it was born. The woman was delivered of a boy, the son who was to rule all the nations with an iron sceptre, and the child was taken straight up to God and to his throne, while the woman escaped into the desert, where God had prepared a place for her to be looked after for twelve hundred and sixty days.

And now war broke out in heaven, when Michael with his angels attacked the dragon. The dragon fought back with his angels, but they were defeated and driven out of heaven. The great dragon, the primeval serpent, known as the devil or Satan, who had led all the world astray, was hurled down to the earth and his angels were hurled down with him. Then I heard a voice shout from heaven, 'Salvation and power and empire for ever have been won by our God, and all authority for his Christ, now that the accuser, who accused our brothers day and night before our God, has been brought down. They have triumphed over him by the blood of the Lamb and by the word to which they bore witness, because even in the face of death they did not cling to life. So let the heavens rejoice and all who live there; but for you, earth and sea, disaster is coming – because the devil has gone down to you in a rage, knowing that he has little time left.'

THE DRAGON, THE BEAST AND THE FALSE PROPHET
Revelation 12:13 – 13:18

As soon as the dragon found himself hurled down to the earth, he sprang in pursuit of the woman, the mother of the male child, but she was given a pair of the great eagle's wings to fly away from the serpent into the desert, to the place where she was to be looked after for a time, two times and half a time. So the serpent vomited water from his mouth, like a river, after the woman, to sweep her away in the current, but the earth came to her rescue; it opened its mouth and swallowed the river spewed from the dragon's mouth. Then the dragon was enraged with the woman and went away to make war on the rest of her children, who obey God's commandments and have in themselves the witness of Jesus.

And I took my stand on the seashore.

Then I saw a beast emerge from the sea: it had seven heads and ten horns, with a coronet on each of its ten horns, and its heads were marked with blasphemous titles. I saw that the beast was like a leopard, with paws like a bear and a mouth like a lion; the dragon had handed over to it his own power and his throne and his immense authority. I saw that one of its heads seemed to have had a fatal wound but that this deadly injury had healed and the whole world had marvelled and followed the beast. They prostrated themselves in front of the dragon because he had given the beast his authority; and they prostrated themselves in front of the beast, saying, 'Who can compare with the beast? Who can fight against it?' The beast was allowed to mouth its boasts and blasphemies and to be active for forty-two months; and it mouthed its blasphemies against God, against his name, his heavenly Tent and all those who are sheltered there. It was allowed to make war against the saints and conquer them, and given power over every race, people, language and nation; and all people of the world will worship it, that is, everybody whose name has not been written down since the foundation of the world in the sacrificial Lamb's book of life. Let anyone who can hear, listen: Those for captivity to captivity; those for death by the sword to death by the sword. This is why the saints must have perseverance and faith.

Then I saw a second beast, emerging from the ground; it had two horns like a lamb, but made a noise like a dragon. This second beast exercised all the power of the first beast, on its behalf making the world and all its people worship the first beast, whose deadly injury had healed. And it worked great miracles, even to calling down fire from heaven onto the earth while people watched. Through the miracles which it was allowed to do on behalf of the first beast, it was able to lead astray the people of the world and persuade them to put up a statue in honour of the beast that had been wounded by the sword and still lived. It was allowed to breathe life into this statue, so that the statue of the beast was able to speak, and to have anyone who refused to worship the statue of the beast put to death. It compelled everyone – small and great alike, rich and poor, slave and citizen – to be branded on the right hand or on the forehead, and made it illegal for anyone to buy or sell anything unless he had been branded with the name of the beast or with the number of its name.

There is need for shrewdness here: anyone clever may interpret the number of the beast: it is the number of a human being, the number 666.

THE HARVEST OF THE EARTH
Revelation 14

Next in my vision I saw Mount Zion, and standing on it the Lamb who had with him a hundred and forty-four thousand people, all with his name and his Father's name written on their foreheads. I heard a sound coming out of heaven like the sound of the ocean or the roar of thunder; it was like the sound of harpists playing their harps. There before the throne they were singing a new hymn in the presence of the four living creatures and the elders, a hymn that could be learnt only by the hundred and forty-four thousand who had been redeemed from the world. These are the sons who have kept their virginity and not been defiled with women; they follow the Lamb wherever he goes; they, out of all people, have been redeemed to be the first-fruits for God and for the Lamb. No lie was found in their mouths and no fault can be found in them.

Then I saw another angel, flying high overhead, sent to announce the gospel of eternity to all who live on the earth, every nation, race, language and tribe. He was calling, 'Fear God and glorify him, because the time has come for him to sit in judgment; worship the maker of heaven and earth and sea and the springs of water.'

A second angel followed him, calling, 'Babylon has fallen,

Babylon the Great has fallen, Babylon which gave the whole world the wine of retribution to drink.'

A third angel followed, shouting aloud, 'All those who worship the beast and his statue, or have had themselves branded on the hand or forehead, will be made to drink the wine of God's fury which is ready, undiluted, in his cup of retribution; in fire and brimstone they will be tortured in the presence of the holy angels and the Lamb and the smoke of their torture rise for ever and ever. There will be no respite, night or day, for those who worship the beast or its statue or accept branding with its name.' This is why there must be perseverance in the saints who keep the commandments of God and faith in Jesus. Then I heard a voice from heaven say to me, 'Write down: Blessed are those who die in the Lord! Blessed indeed, the Spirit says; now they can rest for ever after their work, since their good deeds go with them.'

Now in my vision I saw a white cloud and, sitting on it, one like a son of man with a gold crown on his head and a sharp sickle in his hand. Then another angel came out of the sanctuary and shouted at the top of his voice to the one sitting on the cloud, 'Ply your sickle and reap: harvest time has come and the harvest of the earth is ripe.' Then the one sitting on the cloud set his sickle to work on the earth, and the harvest of earth was reaped.

Another angel, who also carried a sharp sickle, came out of the temple in heaven, and the angel in charge of the fire left the altar and shouted at the top of his voice to the one with the sharp sickle, 'Put your sickle in, and harvest the bunches from the vine of the earth; all its grapes are ripe.' So the angel set his sickle to work on the earth and harvested the whole vintage of the earth and put it into a huge winepress, the winepress of God's anger, outside the city, where it was trodden until the blood that came out of the winepress was up to the horses' bridles as far away as sixteen hundred furlongs.

THE SEVEN PLAGUES
Revelation 15:1 – 16:21

And I saw in heaven another sign, great and wonderful: seven angels were bringing the seven plagues that are the last of all, because they exhaust the anger of God. I seemed to be looking at a sea of crystal suffused with fire, and standing by the lake of glass, those who had fought against the beast and won, and against his statue and the number which is his name. They all had harps from God, and they were singing the hymn of Moses, the servant of God, and the hymn of the Lamb:

> How great and wonderful are all your works,
> Lord God Almighty;
> upright and true are all your ways,
> King of nations.
> Who does not revere and glorify your name, O Lord?
> For you alone are holy,
> and all nations will come and adore you
> for the many acts of saving justice you have shown.

After this, in my vision, the sanctuary, the tent of the Testimony, opened in heaven, and out came the seven angels with the seven plagues, wearing pure white linen, fastened round their waists with belts of gold. One of the four living creatures gave the seven angels seven golden bowls filled with the anger of God who lives for ever and ever. The smoke from the glory and the power of God filled the temple so that no one could go into it until the seven plagues of the seven angels were completed.

Then I heard a loud voice from the sanctuary calling to the seven angels, 'Go, and empty the seven bowls of God's anger over the earth.'

The first angel went and emptied his bowl over the earth; at once, on all the people who had been branded with the mark of the beast and had worshipped its statue, there came disgusting and virulent sores.

The second angel emptied his bowl over the sea, and it turned to blood, like the blood of a corpse, and every living creature in the sea died.

The third angel emptied his bowl into the rivers and springs of water and they turned into blood. Then I heard the angel of water say, 'You are the Upright One, He who is, He who was, the Holy One, for giving this verdict: they spilt the blood of the saints and the prophets, and blood is what you have given them to drink; it is what they deserve.' And I heard the altar itself say, 'Truly, Lord God Almighty, the punishments you give are true and just.'

The fourth angel emptied his bowl over the sun and it was made to scorch people with its flames; but though people were scorched by the fierce heat of it, they cursed the name of God who had the power to cause such plagues, and they would not repent and glorify him.

The fifth angel emptied his bowl over the throne of the beast and its whole empire was plunged into darkness. People were biting their tongues for pain, but instead of repenting for what they had done, they cursed the God of heaven because of their pains and sores.

The sixth angel emptied his bowl over the great river Euphrates; all the water dried up so that a way was made for the kings of the East to come in. Then from the jaws of dragon and beast and false prophet I saw three foul spirits come; they looked like frogs and in fact were demon spirits, able to work miracles, going out to all the kings of the world to call them together for the war of the Great Day of God the Almighty. – Look, I shall come like a thief. Blessed is anyone who has kept watch, and has kept his clothes on, so that he does not go out naked and expose his shame. – They called the kings together at the place called, in Hebrew, Armageddon.

The seventh angel emptied his bowl into the air, and a great voice boomed out from the sanctuary, 'The end has come.' Then there were flashes of lightning and peals of thunder and a violent earthquake, unparalleled since humanity first came into existence. The Great City was split into three parts and the cities of the world collapsed; Babylon the Great was not forgotten: God made her drink the full winecup of his retribution. Every island vanished and the mountains disappeared; and hail, with great hailstones weighing a talent each, fell from the sky on the people. They cursed God for sending a plague of hail; it was the most terrible plague.

THE WHORE OF BABYLON
Revelation 17:1 – 19:10

One of the seven angels that had the seven bowls came to speak to me, and said, 'Come here and I will show you the punishment of the great prostitute who is enthroned beside abundant waters, with whom all the kings of the earth have prostituted themselves, and who has made all the population of the world drunk with the wine of her adultery.' He took me in spirit to a desert, and there I saw a woman riding a scarlet beast which had seven heads and ten horns and had blasphemous titles written all over it. The woman was dressed in purple and scarlet and glittered with gold and jewels and pearls, and she was holding a gold winecup filled with the disgusting filth of her prostitution; on her forehead was written a name, a cryptic name: 'Babylon the Great, the mother of all the prostitutes and all the filthy practices on the earth.' I saw that she was drunk, drunk with the blood of the saints, and the blood of the martyrs of Jesus; and when I saw her, I was completely mystified. The angel said to me, 'Do you not understand? I will tell you the meaning of this woman, and of the beast she is riding, with the seven heads and the ten horns.

'The beast you have seen was once alive and is alive no longer; it is yet to come up from the Abyss, but only to go to its destruction. And the people of the world, whose names have not been written since the beginning of the world in the book of life, will be astonished when they see how the beast was once alive and is alive no longer, and is still to come.

'This calls for shrewdness. The seven heads are the seven hills, on which the woman is sitting. The seven heads are also seven emperors. Five of them have already gone, one is here now, and one is yet to come; once here, he must stay for a short while. The beast, who was alive and is alive no longer, is at the same time the eighth and one of the seven, and he is going to his destruction.

'The ten horns which you saw are ten kings who have not yet been given their royal power but will have royal authority only for a single hour and in association with the beast. They are all of one mind in putting their strength and their powers at the beast's disposal, and they will go to war against the Lamb; but because the Lamb is Lord of lords and King of kings, he will defeat them, he and his followers, the called, the chosen, the trustworthy.'

The angel continued, 'The waters you saw, beside which the prostitute was sitting, are all the peoples, the populations, the nations and the languages. But the ten horns and the beast will turn against the prostitute, and tear off her clothes and leave her stark naked; then they will eat her flesh and burn the remains in the fire. In fact, God has influenced their minds to do what he intends, to agree together to put their royal powers at the beast's disposal until the time when God's words shall be fulfilled. The woman you saw is the great city which has authority over all the rulers on earth.'

After this, I saw another angel come down from heaven, with great authority given to him; the earth shone with his glory. At the top of his voice he shouted, 'Babylon has fallen, Babylon the Great has fallen, and has become the haunt of devils and a lodging for every foul spirit and dirty, loathsome bird. All the nations have drunk deep of the wine of her prostitution; every king on the earth has prostituted himself with her, and every merchant grown rich through her debauchery.'

Another voice spoke from heaven; I heard it say, 'Come out, my people, away from her, so that you do not share in her crimes and have the same plagues to bear. Her sins have reached up to the sky, and God has her crimes in mind: treat her as she has treated others. She must be paid double the amount she exacted. She is to have a doubly strong cup of her own mixture. Every one of her pomps and orgies is to be matched by a torture or an agony. I am enthroned as queen, she thinks; I am no widow and will never know bereavement. For that, in one day, the plagues will fall on her: disease and mourning and famine. She will be burned to the ground. The Lord God who has condemned her is mighty.'

'There will be mourning and weeping for her by the kings of the earth who have prostituted themselves with her and held orgies with her. They see the smoke as she burns, while they keep at a safe distance through fear of her anguish. They will say:

Mourn, mourn for this great city,
Babylon, so powerful a city,
in one short hour your doom has come upon you.

'There will be weeping and distress over her among all the traders of the earth when no one is left to buy their cargoes of goods; their stocks of gold and silver, jewels and pearls, linen and purple and silks and scarlet; all the sandalwood, every piece in ivory or fine wood, in bronze or iron or marble; the cinnamon and spices, the myrrh and ointment and incense; wine, oil, flour and corn; their stocks of cattle, sheep, horses and chariots, their slaves and their human cargo.

'All the fruits you had set your hearts on have failed you; gone for ever, never to return again, is your life of magnificence and ease.

'The traders who had made a fortune out of her will be standing at a safe distance through fear of her anguish, mourning and weeping. They will be saying:

Mourn, mourn for this great city;
for all the linen and purple and scarlet that you wore,
for all your finery of gold and jewels and pearls;
your huge riches are all destroyed within a single hour.

All the captains and seafaring men, sailors and all those who make a living from the sea kept a safe distance, watching the smoke as she burned, and crying out, "Has there ever been a city as great as this!" They threw dust on their heads and said, with tears and groans:

Mourn, mourn for this great city
whose lavish living has made a fortune
for every owner of a sea-going ship,
ruined within a single hour.

'Now heaven, celebrate her downfall, and all you saints, apostles and prophets: God has given judgment for you against her.'

Then a powerful angel picked up a boulder like a great millstone, and as he hurled it into the sea, he said, 'That is how the great city of Babylon is going to be hurled down, never to be seen again.

Never again in you
will be heard the song of harpists and minstrels,
the music of flute and trumpet;
never again will craftsmen of every skill be found in you
or the sound of the handmill be heard;
never again will shine the light of the lamp in you,
never again will be heard in you the voices of bridegroom
and bride.
Your traders were the princes of the earth,
all the nations were led astray by your sorcery.

In her was found the blood of prophets and saints, and all the blood that was ever shed on earth.'

After this I heard what seemed to be the great sound of a huge crowd in heaven, singing, 'Alleluia! Salvation and glory and power to our God! He judges fairly, he punishes justly, and he has condemned the great prostitute who corrupted the earth with her prostitution; he has avenged the blood of his servants which she shed.' And again they sang, 'Alleluia! The smoke of her will rise for ever and ever.' Then the twenty-four elders and the four living creatures threw themselves down and worshipped God seated on his throne, and they cried, 'Amen, Alleluia.'

Then a voice came from the throne; it said, 'Praise our God, you servants of his and those who fear him, small and great alike.' And I heard what seemed to be the voices of a huge crowd, like the sound of the ocean or the great roar of thunder, answering, 'Alleluia! The reign of the Lord our God Almighty has begun; let us be glad and joyful and give glory to God, because this is the time for the marriage of the Lamb. His bride is ready, and she has been able to dress herself in dazzling white linen, because her linen is made of the good deeds of the saints.' The angel said, 'Write this, "Blessed are those who are invited to the wedding feast of the Lamb,"' and he added, 'These words of God are true.' Then I knelt at his feet to worship him, but he said to me, 'Never do that: I am your fellow-servant and the fellow-servant of all your brothers who have in themselves the witness of Jesus. God alone you must worship.' The witness of Jesus is the spirit of prophecy.

THE LAST JUDGMENT
Revelation 19:11 – 20:15

And now I saw heaven open, and a white horse appear; its rider was called Trustworthy and True; in uprightness he judges and makes war. His eyes were flames of fire, and he was crowned with many coronets; the name written on him was known only to himself, his cloak was soaked in blood. He is known by the name, The Word of God. Behind him, dressed in linen of dazzling white, rode the armies of heaven on white horses. From his mouth came a sharp sword with which to strike the unbelievers; he is the one who will rule them with an iron sceptre, and tread out the wine of Almighty God's fierce retribution. On his cloak and on his thigh a name was written: King of kings and Lord of lords.

I saw an angel standing in the sun, and he shouted aloud to all the birds that were flying high overhead in the sky, 'Come here. Gather together at God's great feast. You will eat the flesh of kings, and the flesh of great generals and heroes, the flesh of horses and their riders and of all kinds of people, citizens and slaves, small and great alike.'

Then I saw the beast, with all the kings of the earth and their armies, gathered together to fight the Rider and his army. But the beast was taken prisoner, together with the false prophet who had worked miracles on the beast's behalf and by them had deceived those who had accepted branding with the mark of the beast and those who had worshipped his statue. These two were hurled alive into the fiery lake of burning sulphur. All the rest were killed by the sword of the Rider, which came out of his mouth, and all the birds glutted themselves with their flesh.

Then I saw an angel come down from heaven with the key of the Abyss in his hand and an enormous chain. He overpowered the dragon, that primeval serpent which is the devil and Satan, and chained him up for a thousand years. He hurled him into the Abyss and shut the entrance and sealed it over him, to make sure he would not lead the nations astray again until the thousand years had passed. At the end of that time he must be released, but only for a short while.

Then I saw thrones, where they took their seats, and on them was conferred the power to give judgment. I saw the souls of all who had been beheaded for having witnessed for Jesus and for having preached God's word, and those who refused to worship the beast or his statue and would not accept the brand-mark on their foreheads or hands; they came to life, and reigned with Christ for a thousand years. The rest of the dead did not come to life until the thousand years were over; this is the first resurrection. Blessed and holy are those who share in the first resurrection; the second death has no power over them but they will be priests of God and of Christ and reign with him for a thousand years.

When the thousand years are over, Satan will be released from his prison and will come out to lead astray all the nations in the four quarters of the earth, Gog and Magog, and mobilize them for war, his armies being as many as the sands of the sea. They came swarming over the entire country and besieged the camp of the saints, which is the beloved City. But fire rained down on them from heaven and consumed them.

Then the devil, who led them astray, was hurled into the lake of fire and sulphur, where the beast and the false prophet are, and their torture will not come to an end, day or night, for ever and ever.

Then I saw a great white throne and the One who was sitting on it. In his presence, earth and sky vanished, leaving no trace. I saw the dead, great and small alike, standing in front of his throne while the books lay open. And another book was opened, which is the book of life, and the dead were judged from what was written in the books, as their deeds deserved.

The sea gave up all the dead who were in it; Death and Hades were emptied of the dead that were in them; and every one was judged as his deeds deserved. Then Death and Hades were hurled into the burning lake. This burning lake is the second death; and anybody whose name could not be found written in the book of life was hurled into the burning lake.

THE CELESTIAL CITY
Revelation 21:1 – 22:15

Then I saw a new heaven and a new earth; the first heaven and the first earth had disappeared now, and there was no longer any sea. I saw the holy city, the new Jerusalem, coming down out of heaven from God, prepared as a bride dressed for her husband. Then I heard a loud voice call from the throne, 'Look, here God lives among human beings. He will make his home among them; they will be his people, and he will be their God, God-with-them. He will wipe away all tears from their eyes; there will be no more death, and no more mourning or sadness or pain. The world of the past has gone.'

Then the One sitting on the throne spoke. 'Look, I am making the whole of creation new. Write this, "What I am saying is trustworthy and will come true."' Then he said to me, 'It has already happened. I am the Alpha and the Omega, the Beginning and the End. I will give water from the well of life free to anybody who is thirsty; anyone who proves victorious will inherit these things; and I will be his God and he will be my son. But the legacy for cowards, for those who break their word, or worship obscenities, for murderers and the sexually immoral, and for sorcerers, worshippers of false gods or any other sort of liars, is the second death in the burning lake of sulphur.'

One of the seven angels that had the seven bowls full of the seven final plagues came to speak to me and said, 'Come here and I will show you the bride that the Lamb has married.' In the spirit, he carried me to the top of a very high mountain, and showed me Jerusalem, the holy city, coming down out of heaven from God. It had all the glory of God and glittered like some precious jewel of crystal-clear diamond. Its wall was of a great height and had twelve gates; at each of the twelve gates there was an angel, and over the gates were written the names of the twelve tribes of Israel; on the east there were three gates, on the north three gates, on the south three gates, and on the west three gates. The city walls stood on twelve foundation stones, each one of which bore the name of one of the twelve apostles of the Lamb.

The angel that was speaking to me was carrying a gold measuring rod to measure the city and its gates and wall. The plan of the city is perfectly square, its length the same as its breadth. He measured the city with his rod and it was twelve thousand furlongs, equal in length and in breadth, and equal in height. He measured its wall, and this was a hundred and forty-four cubits high – by human measurements. The wall was built of diamond, and the city of pure gold, like clear glass. The foundations of the city wall were faced with all kinds of precious stone: the first with diamond, the second lapis lazuli, the third turquoise, the fourth crystal, the fifth agate, the sixth ruby, the seventh gold quartz, the eighth malachite, the ninth topaz, the tenth emerald, the eleventh sapphire and the twelfth amethyst. The twelve gates were twelve pearls, each gate being made of a single pearl, and the main street of the city was pure gold, transparent as glass. I could not see any temple in the city since the Lord God Almighty and the Lamb were themselves the temple, and the city did not need the sun or the moon for light, since it was lit by the radiant glory of God, and the Lamb was a lighted torch for it. The nations will come to its light and the kings of the earth will bring it their treasures. Its gates will never be closed by day – and there will be no night there – and the nations will come, bringing their treasure and their wealth. Nothing unclean may come into it: no one who does what is loathsome or false, but only those who are listed in the Lamb's book of life.

Then the angel showed me the river of life, rising from the throne of God and of the Lamb and flowing crystal-clear. Down the middle of the city street, on either bank of the river were the trees of life, which bear twelve crops of fruit in a year, one in each month, and the leaves of which are the cure for the nations.

The curse of destruction will be abolished. The throne of God and of the Lamb will be in the city; his servants will worship him, they will see him face to face, and his name will be written on their foreheads. And night will be abolished; they will not need lamplight or sunlight, because the Lord God will be shining on them. They will reign for ever and ever.

The angel said to me, 'All that you have written is sure and will come true: the Lord God who inspires the prophets has sent his angel to reveal to his servants what is soon to take place. I am coming soon!' Blessed are those who keep the prophetic message of this book.

I, John, am the one who heard and saw these things. When I had heard and seen them all, I knelt at the feet of the angel who had shown them to me, to worship him; but he said, 'Do no such thing: I am your fellow-servant and the fellow-servant of your brothers the prophets and those who keep the message of this book. God alone you must worship.'

This, too, he said to me, 'Do not keep the prophecies in this book a secret, because the Time is close. Meanwhile let the sinner continue sinning, and the unclean continue to be unclean; let the upright continue in his uprightness, and those who are holy continue to be holy. Look, I am coming soon, and my reward is with me, to repay everyone as their deeds deserve. I am the Alpha and the Omega, the First and the Last, the Beginning and the End. Blessed are those who will have washed their robes clean, so that they will have the right to feed on the tree of life and can come through the gates into the city. Others must stay outside: dogs, fortune-tellers, and the sexually immoral, murderers, idolaters, and everyone of false speech and false life.'

EPILOGUE
Revelation 22:16–21

I, Jesus, have sent my angel to attest these things to you for the sake of the churches. I am the sprig from the root of David and the bright star of the morning.

The Spirit and the Bride say, 'Come!' Let everyone who listens answer, 'Come!' Then let all who are thirsty come: all who want it may have the water of life, and have it free.

This is my solemn attestation to all who hear the prophecies in this book: if anyone adds anything to them, God will add to him every plague mentioned in the book; if anyone cuts anything out of the prophecies in this book, God will cut off his share of the tree of life and of the holy city, which are described in the book.

The one who attests these things says: I am indeed coming soon.

Amen; come, Lord Jesus.

May the grace of the Lord Jesus be with you all. Amen.

Index of Primary Sources